THE WORLD OF
PRIMATES

THE WORLD OF
PRIMATES

PATRICK HOOK

GRAMERCY

This 2000 edition is published by Gramercy Books™,
an imprint of Random House Value Publishing, Inc.,
280 Park Avenue, New York, NY 10017,
by arrangement with PRC Publishing Ltd,
Kiln House, 210 New Kings Road, London, SW6 4NZ.

Printed and bound in China

Random House
New York • Toronto • London • Sydney • Auckland
http://www.randomhouse.com/

A catalogue record for this book is available from the Library of Congress.

ISBN 0-517-16204-0

8 7 6 5 4 3 2 1

ACKNOWLEDGMENTS

The publisher wishes to thank the following for supplying the photography for this book:

Pictor International - London for pages 2, 6-7, 12, 17, 41, 68 (top), 101, 103 (bottom), 104, 105, 106-107, 109, 115, 116, 118, 119, 123 and back cover image;
© Jonathan Plant/RSPCA Photolibrary for pages 8 (cut out) and 112-113;
© Richard Hughes/RSPCA Photolibrary for pages 8 (left);
© Anthony Bannister; Gallo Images/CORBIS for pages 9;
© Jonathan Blair/CORBIS for pages 10 (top left);
© John Garrett/CORBIS for pages 10 (top right);
© Andrew Routh/RSPCA Photolibrary for pages 10 (bottom), 21, 23 (bottom), 80 (bottom) and 103 (top);
© E A Janes/RSPCA Photolibrary for front cover image and pages 11, 14 (left), 19 (bottom), 26, 42 (bottom), 60 (detail), 63, 64, 70, 72-73, 84, 85 (top left and right, bottom), 86-87, 95, 97 (top right), 100 (detail), 108, 110-111 and 114;
© Colin Seddon/RSPCA Photolibrary for pages 14-15 (main), 22 (bottom), 23 (top) and 117;
© Picture Press/CORBIS for pages 13;
© Susan Stockwell/RSPCA Photolibrary for pages 16 (left) and 82 (bottom);
© Roger Ressmeyer/CORBIS for pages 18 and 90-91;
Frank Krahmer/© Wild Images Ltd/RSPCA Photolibrary for pages 19 (top);
© Ms Marina Imperi/RSPCA Photolibrary for pages 22 (top);
© Frank Nowikowski/RSPCA Photolibrary for pages 24;
© Birgit Koch/RSPCA Photolibrary for pages 27;
© Kevin Schafer/CORBIS for pages 28, 38 (cut out), 54 (detail), 55, 58 (detail), 59, 66 (detail), 71, 81 and 92-93 (main);
Nick Garbutt/© Wild Images Ltd/RSPCA Photolibrary for pages 31, 39 (and detail, above), 40 (detail), 42 (top), 43, 44, 45, 46, 47, 48 (detail), 49 (both), 50 (and detail, above) and 51;
© Galen Rowell/CORBIS for pages 33;
© Jeremy Horner/CORBIS for pages 34;
© Hulton-Deutsch Collection/CORBIS for pages 37;
© Clive Druett; Papilio/CORBIS for pages 38 (left);
Tim Martin/© Wild Images Ltd/RSPCA Photolibrary for pages 52 (detail) and 53 (both);
© Clem Haagner; Gallo Images/CORBIS for pages 56 (detail) and 57;
© Terry Whittaker; Frank Lane Picture Agency/CORBIS for pages 61, 83, 124 and 127;
© Stuart Westmorland/CORBIS for pages 65 (main);
Stephen Packham/© Wild Images Ltd/RSPCA Photolibrary for pages 65 (right) and 67;
Martin Dohrn/© Wild Images Ltd/RSPCA Photolibrary for pages 68 (bottom) and 77;
© Mike Lane/RSPCA Photolibrary for pages 74 (detail), 79 and 125;
© Geoff du Feu/RSPCA Photolibrary for pages 80 (top);
© Philip Sharpe/RSPCA Photolibrary for pages 82 (top);
© Vanessa Latford/RSPCA Photolibrary for pages 88 and 89;
© Richard Thompson/RSPCA Photolibrary for pages 93 (right);
© Uwe Walz/CORBIS for pages 94 (detail) and 96;
© Philip Marazzi/CORBIS for pages 97 (top left and bottom);
© Kevin R Morris/CORBIS for pages 98-99;
© Klaus-Peter Wolf/RSPCA for pages 120-121;
John Downer/© Wild Images Ltd/RSPCA for pages 122.

CONTENTS

PART 1

PART 2

PART**ONE**

INTRODUCTION

Above: The other major grouping of primates is the "Haplorhini"—which includes an incredibly diverse range of families, from marmosets to the humans and great apes, such as this chimpanzee.

Right: There are over 230 different species of primates—the grouping known as the "Strepsirhini" includes many nocturnal ones, such as this lesser bushbaby.

The primates are a large, diverse, and interesting group of animals, consisting of over 230 different species. They include not only the well-known monkeys, apes, and man, but also many smaller creatures such as the bushbabies and lemurs. The primates are all mammals—which means they belong to the Class Mammalia. The scientific name for the grouping of the primates themselves is the Order Primata. This can then be further split into two more categories—the "Strepsirhini" and the "Haplorhini."

The Strepsirhini include such families as the lemurs, lorises, pottos and bushbabies. The Haplorhini includes such families as the marmosets, tamarins, New World monkeys, Old World monkeys, gibbons, great apes, and humans. There was a time when the Tree shrews (*Scandentia*) and the flying lemurs (*Dermoptera*) were included in the primate order, but this has been out of use for a very long time now. This is because a lot more is now known about how various animals are related to one another, and it has become clear that these animals are too far distant.

While there are lots of different ecological niches occupied by the many species of primates, they are all omnivores—that is both animal and vegetable matter form part of their diets. The extent to which they consume different foodstuffs varies considerably—some, such as the gorilla, are almost entirely vegetarian (herbivorous), while others, such as the slender loris are much more biased towards eating insects and small vertebrates.

The smallest primates are the mouse lemurs, which may weigh as little as two ounces when fully grown; the largest are the huge silverback male gorillas, which can reach 600 pounds! The smaller members of the order have a tail, and in some South American species, such as the spider and capuchin monkeys, it is prehensile—so they can grip with it, allowing them to do things like use it to hang off branches, and so on.

One of the major features of primates is that they have "binocular" vision—that is, they have their eyes set together on the front of the face. The significance of this is that they can judge distance very accurately—imagine trying to jump from one tree to another without knowing exactly how far away the next branch is! These forward-facing eyes are protected by a ring of bone—in early humans the eyebrow was a substantial ridge; this has all but disappeared in modern man.

Humans are spread throughout the world, even occupying Antarctica, albeit on a temporary basis. The non-human primates, however, are mainly restricted to the tropical areas of the world, although there are

Above: All primates are omnivorous—that is, they will all eat both animal and plant matter. Some, such as gorillas, are almost entirely vegetarian, but most will eat a wide variety of foodstuffs—including leaves and fruit.

Top Right: The sizes of the different species of primates vary considerably—as can be seen here, this fully grown lesser mouse lemur is tiny, weighing at most only two or three ounces.

Above Right: The largest of the primates are the silverback male gorillas, which can reach 600 pounds in weight. This one is patiently overseeing some youngsters who are playing at his feet.

some which range into the colder regions. The classic example of this is with the Japanese macaque in the mountainous parts of northern Japan: they are famous for staying warm in the winter by soaking themselves in hot volcanic pools! The reason that primates are more or less restricted to the tropics is attributed to the fact that they cannot find enough food to survive through the cold winters of non-tropical regions. Most other mammals either hibernate or migrate to warmer climes to avoid the ravages of winter.

EVOLUTION

The subject of primate evolution can arouse all sorts of responses in scientists, particularly taxonomists (these are people who put species into different groups according to anatomical features). This is because, whatever generalizations you make about primates, you inherently include humans. In the last century, passions reached fever pitch when an eminent scientist at a major convention suggested that man was descended from the ape. One cynical observer asked whether this was on his mother's or his father's side of the family!

These days, we can demonstrate a reasonably complete fossil record from ape to man, although there are a few gaps which diminish with every new find. The religious perspective is that God created man, the view of most biologists is that all primates owe their descent to a single ancestral mammal—a small tree shrew-like creature whose ancestors in turn date back more than 110 million years.

Above: The view of most modern scientists is that man is descended from the apes. This orangutan, however, seems more evolved than many humans I've met . . .

ANATOMY

Above: It is clear from the briefest of glimpses that there is thought going on behind these eyes! This orangutan has binocular vision—that is, its eyes are positioned on the front of its face.

Right: The eyes of nocturnal primates are huge in comparison to those which are active during the day. The slender loris is a fine example of this—it hunts its prey by stealth in almost total darkness, creeping up on beetles, lizards and other small creatures before pouncing on them at great speed.

From the common starting point of the tree shrew-like ancestor, there are many physical structures that are now shared throughout the primate order. These include hands which are able to grasp objects; a key feature is the fact that the thumb is "opposite" the fingers—the ultimate dexterity in this respect is demonstrated by humans. The fingers are also more specialized than those of non-primates, having sensitive pads protected by fingernails and toenails. These allow for much more delicate control when handling objects, which can be important for all sorts of tasks from social grooming to collecting food. The structure of primate arms is also common throughout the order, although many have specific specializations to facilitate swinging through trees at great speed.

The features of the head are fundamental to what separates the primates from all other animals—they all have binocular vision, although the more "primitive" examples, such as the lemurs, don't have their eyes on the front of the face like the more highly evolved ones such as chimpanzees and humans. The eyes themselves are very highly developed, having for instance, color vision. They are also protected by ridges of bone—we humans call them cheekbones and eyebrows.

The nocturnal primates have tremendously specialized eyes, being able to see well in what humans would consider almost total darkness. For a start, their eyes are much bigger, allowing them to capture much more of the available light. Their pupils also open up more for the same reason. The retina—onto which the light is focused, is made up of "rods and cones." These are the receptor cells that turn the light into nerve impulses, which are then sent to the brain. The cones are used for bright light, and the rods for darker conditions. In nocturnal animals, including those that are primates, the number of cones is reduced considerably, and the proportion of rods is increased dramatically. This means that they may be able to see extremely well at night, but pretty poorly in daytime.

Most nocturnal animals also have other features that allow them to see even better at night—one of these is the "tapetum," a thin membrane that acts as a sort of internal mirror, capturing any light which was not absorbed by the retina, and reflecting it back for a second chance to be detected.

The brain is obviously a key element of the head; it is where all the sensory inputs are integrated and analyzed in order to produce responses to various stimuli. In primates the sense of smell is much reduced—this has been sacrificed in order to improve the processing of visual information. As a consequence of this, the nose or "snout" is much smaller than, say, those of dogs or mice. The brain in primates is very much bigger for their body size than almost all other animals, although in whales and dolphins they are also remarkably big.

Right: This chimpanzee hand tells us many things—it has fingernails and knuckles that are very similar to those of humans.

Below: Even though this gorilla has huge nostrils, the sense of smell in primates is much less acute than that of many other mammals, such as dogs, cats, or mice. The reason for this is that evolution has rearranged the brain to process more visual information instead.

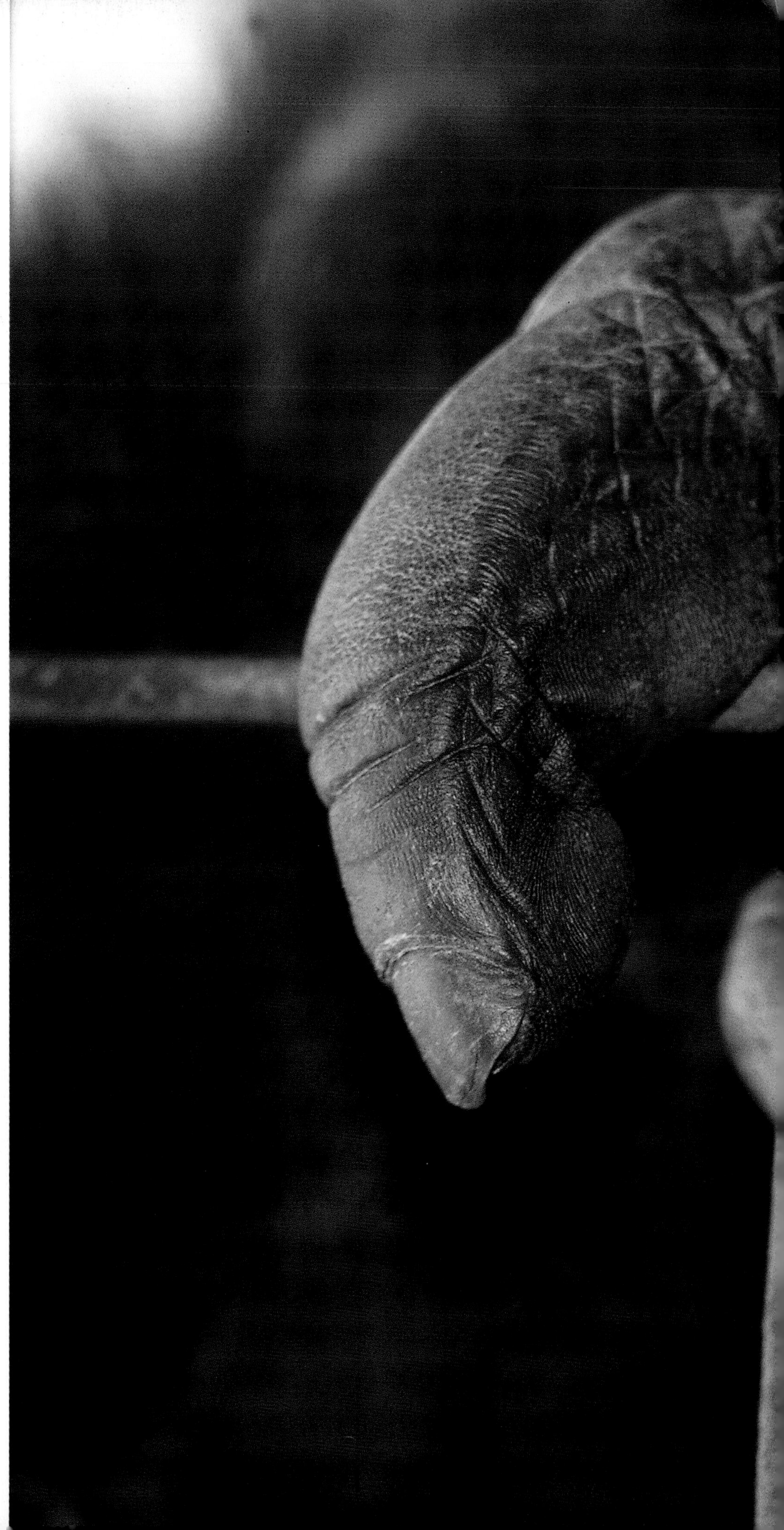

BEHAVIOR

Above: The highly evolved behaviors of primate societies is in part due to the long periods of care and nurture of their young. This is a heavy investment on the part of the parents—this young savannah baboon seems to be getting plenty of devoted love and attention!

Right: Facial expressions are an inherent part of primate communication—this orangutan is demonstrating that rather well!

The consequence of having a highly developed brain is that behavior becomes much more complex. Primates have many behavioral patterns in common, such as being arboreal, that is, tree-dwelling—although some have developed into being partly or wholly terrestrial. Having a brain that is capable of working out complicated issues has meant that many primates are excellent opportunists, being able to take advantage of situations that they may well have not met before. This gives them a competitive advantage over animals which have smaller brains, meaning that they can out-breed them, or just simply survive during harsh times where the others could not.

An example of the mental/physical integration of the primate structure is that of tool use. The brain is capable of working out that a situation could be resolved by the use of a tool of some description—superb manual dexterity and hand/eye co-ordination often allow them to achieve it. An excellent illustration is when chimpanzees use small sticks to extract termites from tiny holes in their mounds, or when they use handfuls of leaves to soak up water from otherwise inaccessible places.

One of the consequences of having large brains and complex behaviors is that social issues also become very complicated, and often very advanced. The ultimate example of social organization is, of course, that of humans, but many primate species also have tremendously involved societal relationships. This is inextricably linked to the care and nurture of offspring, which are dependent on at least one parent for very long periods in comparison to almost all other animals. This dependency is not all bad though, for it means that parental teaching can be much more detailed than if the offspring were independent at an earlier age.

Another facet of social relationships that is of major importance in primates is that of communication between individuals or groups. This can take the form of vocalizations, smells, colors, gestures, body attitudes, and most of all, especially in humans, facial expressions. These signals can indicate all sorts of things, such as fear, anger, jealousy, sexual arousal, excitement, territory demarcation, and so on. This is such a complicated issue that entire books have been written on the subject.

The issue of independent thought in primates is one which psychologists have been debating for years, and will doubtless continue to do so for many more. Some would argue that the ultimate extension of this is that great apes should qualify for the status of "personhood"—that is they should have their own rights under law. There is also the concept of "group consciousness," bandied about using the example of the snow monkeys of Koshima Island, off Japan. In 1952, a small group of these macaques were given some sweet potatoes to eat. One of members started washing them, and the others copied her. The same thing happened when they were given rice mixed with sand—the same monkey

Above: Having large brains means that primates can be excellent opportunists—often taking advantage of situations that other animals could not. Here a Japanese macaque—sometimes called the "Snow Monkey," is keeping itself warm by the snow-covered mountains by sitting in the waters of a hot volcanic spring.

threw it into some water, and scooped off the grains after the sand had sunk. This behavior has been passed on through the subsequent generations, establishing clearly the presence of culture in these macaques.

This much is not questioned; however, not long afterwards, a similar group on the mainland started doing the same thing. There are those who argue that this demonstrates "group consciousness," and that some form of telepathy was at work, brought about by the large numbers of animals thinking similar thoughts. Others believe that it illustrates how clever the primate mind is—given a problem and a potential solution, sooner or later (usually sooner), some individual will work out the answer.

Much research has been conducted into the abilities of primates to understand concepts such as "self," "want," and "know." To this end, many have been taught sign language, often producing remarkable results. One of the problems with demonstrating abstract thought, however, is that it is very difficult to show that an answer to a question which appears to show deep understanding is not merely a random chance response rather than a conditioned response.

The most successful sign language experiments have been with gorillas and chimpanzees, some of whom have demonstrated the ability to understand humor, embarrassment, grieving, sadness, and many other very advanced emotional states. Unfortunately, most of the results are open to interpretation—it can be only too easy for some critic to rubbish many years of work of a dedicated researcher, simply by saying that it could be chance, or that a particular response was simple mimicking. My own view, having worked with many different species of primates, is that they are much more intelligent than they are generally given credit for—maybe the critics should spend more time with the animals, and less time in the classroom!

Above: Some people question whether primates have independent thought. Few individuals who have worked with, or lived in close proximity to, animals such as this Hamadryas baboon have any doubts at all.

Left: It is very hard to determine what an animal is thinking—some people argue against the ability of primates to understand things like humor. This old female Orangutan looks like she knows how to enjoy a good laugh, though!

RESEARCH

Right: Surely the best way to study wild animals is in their natural habitat, away from the constraints of cages, forced diets, and the imposition of unknown group members. In some situations, it can be reasonably easy to observe them, such as here in Rwanda, where you can see the mountain gorillas from quite a distance. More often it is not as easy as this, and you find that the species you wish to observe lives somewhere like the canopy of a rain forest, which could easily be 200 feet above you. The best way in this circumstance is to build observation platforms, and learn to be very, very patient!

DISEASES OF NON-HUMAN PRIMATES

Primates suffer from an extraordinary range of diseases—think of the number that humans suffer from, and add to this considerably. Some major diseases of mankind first started out as diseases of non-human primates—to this day people are still arguing over whether AIDS spread to humans from African monkeys. Another disease that kills humans is monkeypox, which is not far removed from smallpox. Smallpox used to be a major killer of humans, and was eradicated from the entire global population in 1980. However, monkeypox still occurs sporadically in tropical Central and West Africa, where it kills many people, especially the very young. It is usually caused by contact with infected monkeys or squirrels, either through a bite or through contaminated blood.

It is thought that monkeypox is becoming more virulent, spreading further with each major outbreak. This is a major cause for concern, as people are no longer immunized against smallpox, which previously would have provided adequate protection. There are many other diseases held within the non-human primate population that could well spread to humans, so this is a major justification for research work in this area. The problem is, that this raises the issue of whether primates should be used as research tools.

FIELD RESEARCH

One of the most interesting methods of research into primates is performed in the "field," that is, in the wild. This can take many forms, from straightforward exploration and documentation of an area's primate species, through to the detailed recording of a particular group, or even a specific individual's movements and behavior over a period of time.

Both ends of the spectrum of field-work have their merits and rewards, especially when new discoveries are made. The most exciting of these is when new species are found; usually this is in extremely remote areas which have not been explored thoroughly before. This is not always the case though—in recent years a new species called the dwarf marmoset (*Callithrix humilis*) was discovered in Brazil, just a short plane hop from one of its largest cities.

One of the tragedies of the modern era is that, with so much of the planet being deforested, we are losing vast areas of wilderness that have not even been properly explored yet. We are undoubtedly making plant and animal species extinct before we even know that they exist. The fact that we are still discovering species as distinctive as primates demonstrates that there is still much to be found.

PRIMATES IN CAPTIVITY

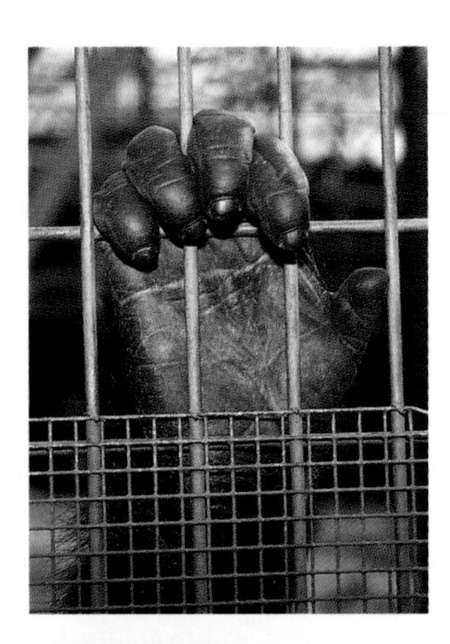

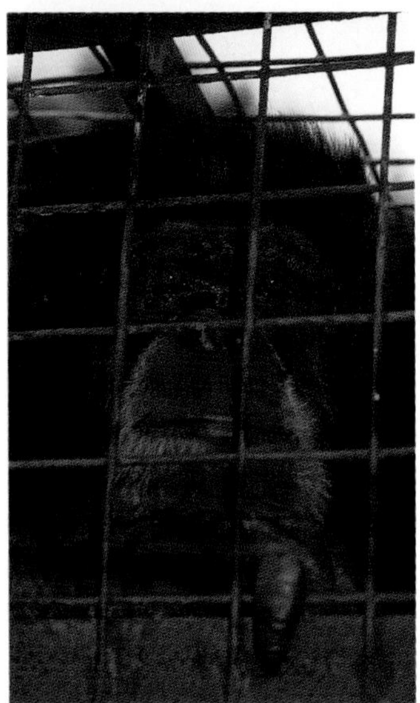

Top: When the discussion turns to primates in captivity, this picture, for me at least, says it all.

Above: Any discussion as to whether primates should be held in captivity will almost certainly arouse fierce debate. I think that it's pretty obvious that this chimpanzee has a clear opinion about being kept locked up in a cage.

Whether or not apes and monkeys (or indeed, any animal) should be held in captivity at all is a major issue—very few people are without a firm view. To try and be dispassionate when discussing animal captivity is difficult, but I am going to try. On the one hand, you have those who argue in favor; their logic usually ties in with one or more of the following: primates are vital for medical research; primates can be indispensable to disabled people as assistants; primates can make good pets, or captive breeding is vital to ensure the survival of critically endangered species.

The arguments against are usually much simpler, and hold that no primate should be held in captivity, and that they belong in the wild where their immediate ancestors lived. There is a mid-way path to this which is where I think my views lie: under exceptional circumstances captivity is justifiable. The problem is, however, that with the clever use of emotions and statistics you can justify almost anything. My perspective is that captive breeding is often the only way to ensure that the most endangered species have any chance of survival.

I personally don't like the use of any animals for any kind of medical research. It is claimed that less than 0.3% of all animal experimentation is carried out on primates, but in my view this still doesn't make it okay. It is, however, very hard to reconcile this attitude to someone who has say, a young daughter whose only hope of surviving an illness is through the testing of new medical procedures on an animal. I think that technology may well be the way forward from this untenable situation—before long we will have "virtual" humans, on which we can do all our testing. These would be computer-generated models of the human body, which were so accurate, right down to the finest chemical detail, that we could perform surgical or pharmaceutical testing on them with complete confidence in the results. This may sound like wild fantasy, but it is not that far off—we can do most of it already.

When there is a situation where primates need to be held in captivity, there are many important issues which need to be addressed if they are to thrive. In many countries, there are specified regulations that spell out in minute detail just how this should be done, especially if it is in the name of medical research. These issues are vital to the well-being of the captives, and include such things as:

Size and construction of cages Are they big enough, and do they take into account the specific requirements for the species, such as height, width, etc? It is also of paramount importance to ensure that any materials used, especially paints, are non-toxic, and pose no other threats to the captives. If there is any risk of injury through falling, floor coverings should be soft. Species that normally live in hollow tree trunks, for instance, should be provided with suitable nest boxes for them to sleep in.

Above: These pictures of a chimpanzee in captivity is a good example of how confinement can affect animals. It has an empty, listless look. There is no hope, and nothing to interest it. It doesn't have to be this way. There are some justifiable reasons for captivity, such as when trying to save a species from extinction through a breeding program, or when you are dealing with sick or rescued animals. If this is the case, then keeping their spirits high is vital to their well-being—large well-appointed spaces are one of the prerequisites, along with expert care and attention.

Left: In my opinion, this is where an animal belongs—in its natural habitat, where it is wild and free. This is a mountain gorilla in the Parc des Volcans, Rwanda, central Africa.

Location of the cages The occupants should be able to access outside areas, and where they are able to do so, care must be taken that there is adequate shelter from sunlight, wind, rain, or any other factors that could be injurious.

Environmental conditions It is important to ensure that they have the right levels of light, heat, humidity, etc. An animal that is held in conditions that are too cold or too dark, for instance, is going to get sick a lot sooner than one that is happy with its situation. The best way to give an animal the right conditions is to mimic as closely as possible its natural habitat.

Cage layout The cages should have suitable plants and trees situated in a manner relevant to the captives. The use of any such vegetation should be carefully considered before it is introduced—it could well be toxic, so expert advice is needed. The structure of any materials used for climbing, swinging or jumping should constitute a reasonable simulation of what the species would encounter in its natural habitat. If it is possible to do so, it is a good idea to move some of these materials around to change the layout every now and again.

Group sizes Solitary animals should not be housed in multiples, and social animals should not be held in solitary confinement. Potential aggression between individuals must be taken into consideration in advance of their being housed together, or losses through injury or stress will be inevitable. Signs of stress include aberrant behavior, and may be immediately obvious, such as when they pull their own hair out (although this could also be a skin problem, such as mites). If there is any doubt, medical attention should be sought.

Stimulation Will the animals be bored with their situation, or will they be provided with suitable activities, such as foraging and play? An excellent way of encouraging animals to maintain an interest in life is to hide their food, forcing them to search for it. Another way is to release live insects into their cages, although it is important to ensure that any that escape cannot be harmful in any way.

Diet Not surprisingly, this is one of the most important issues. Any food or drink supplied should be of the best quality only, and should meet exactly the requirements of the species. Just like humans, though, some individuals will reject what they are meant to eat, and demand something else entirely. Then the next day, they will completely change their minds. This can be a sign of boredom—to get around this, some establishments

implement the idea of a "starve day," where the animals are not fed for all or part of a day. The idea is that it removes any complacency they have about where the next meal is coming from, and encourages them to search any nooks and crannies for morsels of food, just as they would do in the wild. It may sound cruel, but some of the most healthy captive animals I have seen were kept under this regime.

Cleanliness Cages must be kept in such a manner as to remove the possibility of illness through hygiene problems. Any bedding or floor coverings should be easily removable so that it can be changed regularly. Food containers need to be thoroughly cleaned every time they are changed, and should be sited away from overhead structures such that they cannot be contaminated by droppings or urine. The control of pests is also vital—they can carry all sorts of diseases, especially rats, which can contaminate foodstuffs and water supplies.

Safety This is important both for the captives, and for any staff that may come into contact with them. One of the most common ways in which injuries occur—both to staff and the animal concerned—is when an animal is being moved, either from one cage to another, or from one site to another. There are many reasons for this, not the least of which is that the animal may well be very frightened by what is going on, and thus become much more aggressive than usual. A lot of injuries also occur during routine cleaning and maintenance, especially when the staff is new or over-worked.

Staff care and training The level of care and competence shown by staff looking after any animals is fundamental to their well-being. You can have the best facilities in the world, but you also need keepers who really care about the animals.

Monitoring It is important to monitor the health and well-being of any animals in captivity. In the wild it is amazing just how well animals can recover from terrible injuries, but they do not cope well with sickness. This applies even more so in captivity—if an animal gets sick, it should have medical attention immediately.

Above Left: A good supply of clean water is vital to the well-being of any animal, be it in captivity or in the wild, as with this Javan macaque.

Left: Animals that naturally live in social groups should not be held alone—this is exactly analogous to solitary confinement in humans. Likewise, species that would normally be solitary should not be forced into living with other individuals—it is a certain recipe for health problems, be they physical or emotional. These Vervet monkeys are where they should be—in the wild, but if there were a good reason to confine them, it should be in a group such as this.

CONSERVATION

Above: Countless numbers of primates are killed every year by humans—many are used as food, although some supply the gruesome trade in skins or body parts for tourism or traditional medicines.

THE NEGATIVE SIDE

The conservation of endangered primates is an issue that should concern us all. It has been estimated by conservation experts that about half the species of primates alive today are in a state where their very existence is threatened. When a species goes extinct, that's it—it is lost forever. Of the threatened ones, something like one in five is thought to be critically endangered. There are many reasons why this is so—but the root cause for all of them is mankind. As we continue to desecrate the wild places of the planet, we are reducing the places where wild animals can survive. The primary problem is that of deforestation—in many countries the pressure for new living space for humans is so great that even central governments cannot stop the flow of peasant farmers into the forests, where they slash and burn their way through virgin territory.

In many places, the slash and burn policy is exacerbated by the logging and mining industries, which build roads deep into areas that were previously unpenetrated by any humans except the indigenous tribespeople. These highways are used initially for commercial reasons—to extract the truckloads of timber and mineral ores. It does not take long, however, for the peasant farmers to catch up, and when they do, it gives them access to fresh areas in which to plant their crops.

The biggest problem with this is that the policy of cutting down the trees and then burning everything to the ground not only destroys large tracts of priceless forest, but only sustains the farmer for a few months at most. The soil is not deep enough to grow more than one season's worth of plants, so the farmer must then move on, and destroy another piece of land. What he leaves behind is a legacy of death—not only has he killed off all the plants and animals that relied on the original forest to survive, but his handiwork continues to wreak a terrible price for the ecosystem.

After the farmer has given up on the patch of land, the tropical downpours that are characteristic of all rain forests wash away the soil, leaving bare rock. This means that the forest cannot regenerate. Not only is this a tragedy, but when the soil reaches the waterways, it pollutes them, especially if it contains heavy metal deposits. The combination of mud and pollutants are guaranteed to cause problems for any aquatic life in the fresh waters downstream—the action of clouding up the previously clear waters alone is enough to kill most life there very quickly.

The problems with deforestation in South America are probably those best-known to us in the West. However, it is also critically endangering enormous areas in China, Vietnam, throughout the Indo-Malay peninsula, West Africa, and Madagascar, as well as in Colombia, Brazil, and other neighboring countries.

It is a massively difficult problem to overcome—in many third-world countries, commercial greed is backed up by corruption at the highest government levels. The practical reality of this is that many countries which have signed up to conservation treaties are unable to live up to the promises they have made, because their own ministers are being paid off to allow mining or logging companies to continue working illegally. There is also the problem that there are many war-zones, where there is corruption on a massive scale among the military forces, who are paid to oversee the commercial destruction of further priceless forests—many of the vitally important hardwood trees can be worth huge sums of money to industry, but many critically endangered species rely entirely on their presence to survive. This has been a major problem in the troubled forested areas of Laos, Cambodia, and northern Thailand.

There are also many other sources of trouble for endangered primates. In many poor countries, they are being illegally hunted to extinction for their meat. This is particularly so in the tropical forests of central and western Africa, where marauding bands of semi-military men—many of whom are drop-outs from regional conflicts—keep themselves in profit by killing threatened species. These include all the African apes—gorillas, chimpanzees, and bonobos, which are being killed at a rate of somewhere around 5,000 a year. In many areas, this is a greater threat to their survival than the loss of their habitat through deforestation.

The only way to even attempt to slow this tide of slaughter is a two-stage process: first, to give the local people good reasons to not get involved, and second, to give them further reasons to work actively to prevent it occurring at all. One of the ways to do this is through vested interests—to give them a stake in ecotourism, for instance. If they can make a good living by being part of a trade where visitors come to see their local apes, then they are not going to support anyone who wants to butcher these animals for their meat.

An inherent part of this fight-back is through education—and that is where modern technology is able to help; many remote areas are being connected to the internet via satellite systems. It only takes one computer per school to provide huge amounts of information to large numbers of people. Intelligently used, this can be a tremendously powerful way of providing up-to-the-minute news and educational material. Another excellent tool in the quest for large-scale education in remote areas is the clockwork radio. This was designed and produced by an eccentric British inventor by the name of Trevor Baylis—it was his brainchild to provide a way of powering a radio in places where a set of batteries would cost the equivalent of a month's wages.

It is not only in African countries where primates are being hunted for food: the Taiwanese have developed a taste for eating the brains of rare species such as Indonesian Sulawesi macaques (*Macaca nigra*). Horrifically, they eat the brains while the hapless young monkeys are still alive.

The list of human atrocities against animals in general, and primates in particular, is almost endless. The souvenir trade is yet another example of the needless slaughter of helpless creatures perpetrated by mankind. It has been made illegal to import such things as monkey skulls in many "civilized" countries, but even so, species such as the crab-eating macaque and the pig-tailed macaque are continuing to be killed to support an entirely needless trade in dead animals for use in traditional medicines which continues to be a big threat to many species of primates, particularly wherever there is a large Chinese community.

Another of the big problems that many remote parts of the world have to deal with is the demand for energy—usually electricity. One thing that the rain forests of the world have plenty of (so far) is rain—this makes these areas attractive to those who want to establish hydro-electric schemes. When there is a natural water course such as a large waterfall, the impact on the environment may not be that great if a generating plant was installed. Sadly, though, this is rarely the case, and the energy produced is not enough to satisfy the needs of industry. The usual answer is to build an enormous dam, and then to use the flow of water through it to generate massive quantities of energy. This inevitably has terrible consequences for the local environment though—the amount of land that gets flooded for these large-scale projects is staggering. The number of animals and plants that drown is a tragedy. Fortunately, the political desire to implement schemes like major dam projects is waning

There are ways for those of us in the West to help conserve threatened species in far-away countries. An example is the Great Ape Conservation Act of 1999, which was introduced to the United States Senate by Senator Jim Jeffords, which provides financial support to countries starting conservation schemes for great apes. This is the sort of action that is needed throughout the entire planet if we stand any chance of turning the tide of species endangerment.

THE POSITIVE SIDE

The story of conservation is not all doom and gloom—there are many projects around the world which are seeking to protect certain species, and in some cases they are even reintroducing them successfully. An example of such primate conservation, is the cotton-top tamarin (*Saguinus oedipus*), which is one of the most endangered primate species in the world. It came close to extinction because it was discovered that it was a very good model for human biomedical research—something like 30,000 were captured and taken to the United States between 1965 and 1973 alone. Fortunately, its exportation was then made illegal, as its endangered status was finally recognized. This charming little monkey is only found in Colombia, where even though it is no

Most lemurs enjoy basking in the early morning sun—ring-tailed lemurs are no exception to this, as this individual is demonstrating. They are apt to look somewhat comical when they sit like this!

longer captured for research purposes, it is still threatened by the ogre of deforestation. This species made its way into my heart when I helped nurse one that had been neglected in a zoo—with a lot of care and the correct nutrition, she was soon leaping about and showing a lot of interest in life. Sadly the cotton-top tamarin is still being traded, even though Colombia has a ban in place—when there is money to be made criminals will always get involved. Most are smuggled out of the country for the pet trade, often through countries like Panama.

One of the best ways to reverse the drop in numbers of species such as the cotton-top tamarin is to reintroduce them through captive-breeding programs. A vital ingredient in such schemes is having enough knowledge about the animal concerned in order to be able to make the project a success. It is therefore extremely important to know what influences things like breeding success—to this end detailed studies are necessary before good results can be achieved. An example of such a study is "Proyecto Titi" in Colombia, which also encompasses an effective education program both in the USA and in Colombia. Proyecto Titi has been very successful in stimulating the interest of many people, but perhaps most importantly, in those who live locally. They have been taken out into the rain forests, and shown what is happening, what the threats are, and just how the cotton-top tamarin needs their help.

It is through such work that the cotton-top tamarin has a chance of long-term survival. These people need our support, both financially and practically—it is up to us to do so if we want to help stop the destruction of the animals and plants of our planet.

PRIMATES IN MYTHOLOGY

Right: There are many legends from the Indian sub-continent involving monkeys—it's not hard to see why when you see the proximity in which many people there live with them. This old Nepalese man clearly has a long-term companion!

Non-human primates do not play a big role in early western mythology—but this should not be a surprise considering that most legends and myths arose in pagan times, in regions where monkeys were not generally known to exist. It was not until the rise of Christianity that the main source of western cultural influences shifted away from the Greco-Roman empires, and down into the Middle East, where apes and monkeys were more common. In the eastern cultures, however, monkeys had been central to myths and legends for many thousands of years—possibly even tens of thousands of years.

One of the most famous of eastern legends is that of the Monkey-King, based on the life of a famous Chinese monk, Xuan Zang, who lived 602–664 AD. His achievement was to travel on foot across China, and down into India, where he sought the Buddhist holy book, called the Sutra. He then walked all the way back to China, where he produced the first Chinese translations of the Sutra—this was an important event in the history of Chinese Buddhism.

This legend tells of a cheeky, but immensely clever monkey, born from an egg made of stone. He goes through many trials and tribulations—first he becomes king of all the monkeys on Earth, but finds that this is not enough for his ego. He is jealous of the gods, and wants to share in their powers and immortality. By causing such trouble on Earth, Monkey convinces the King of Heaven that only by offering him a position in heaven, can he be kept under control. Once there, he breaks into the heavenly orchard, and steals some of the fruit of immortality. He also tries to steal the wife of one of the other gods, and gets involved in a fight with her husband. This causes immense damage to the palace, and Monkey has to escape the wrath of the Jade Emperor by fleeing back to Earth. Monkey is finally caught and Buddha imprisons him under the rocks of a mountain so massive, that even with his strength and cunning, he cannot escape.

A monk called Tripitaka releases him 500 years later, and he rejoins the world. The price of his freedom is to accompany the monk on a dangerous journey, during which they meet various situations and events that test their strength and endurance. Each of these teaches Monkey important lessons, such as discipline, self-restraint and humility. During this time, Monkey changes from being a self-centered and greedy figure into an honorable disciple to the monk—it is the symbolism of this enlightenment that makes the legend so important in the history of Buddhism.

There are also many legends involving monkeys from the Indian sub-continent. Most of them are centered around the monkey being a bridegroom or lover—sometimes the monkey becomes the equivalent of the western "prince turned into a frog." Whereas the Monkey-King is telling the story of enlightenment, and the fight against feudal rule, the stories from the Indian region seem to be more aimed at the caste system,

Monkeys weren't generally known in the West until historical times, whereas in the East, humans had lived alongside them for tens of thousands of years. Here, at the temple of Koodal Alagar, this monkey seems very much at home.

where people are not allowed to have romantic involvements with those outside their class level.

One of these folk tales tells the story of a monkey-boy born into a large family. His brothers reject and bully him, but by a process of hard work and sharp wits, he overcomes his limitations, and becomes successful and rich. Eventually he decides that he must find himself a wife, so he sets off on a long search; after all, no ordinary girl would be interested in having a monkey for a husband! After a long trip, he finds some girls bathing, so he picks up the cloth belonging to one of them and runs up a tree with it. When she asks for it back, he says that he will do so only if she agrees to marry him. She talks to him, and becomes bewitched by his charm, finally agreeing to go home with him. Her family chases after them, but as his village is so faraway, they are soon left behind. Back at home everyone is amazed that he has found a wife, but they are both made welcome, and live long and happy lives.

Ape-Man Legends

One issue that is bound to raise an animated discussion in any group of people is that whether there are any undiscovered great apes left in the world. In the United States there is the legend of "Bigfoot" and "Sasquatch." In the Himalayas there is the "Yeti" (translates as "magical creature") or as we know it in the West, the "Abominable Snowman." In South America there is another legendary giant ape, known as *Ameranthropoides loysi*, or Mono Rei, and in Malaysia, there is the Orang

Kubu. It seems that in almost every region of the world there is a culture of such legends.

The Yeti has been reported for many years—the first western report was in 1832—and has been the subject of several scientific search missions. It is said to be covered in fur, and about six feet or so in height, only coming out at night, when it hunts yaks and sheep. The local villagers high in the mountainous regions have a long history of sightings of this wildman, and believe that it is a shy creature that communicates by making whistling sounds. Italian climber Reinhold Messner claims to have bought a yeti skeleton from nomads—but he is not allowing anyone to examine it until his book is published. He also claims to have come face to face with yeti four times, and to have taken photographs of them. The yeti sightings have taken place across a vast area—from the Himalayas that are traditionally taken to be its home, across Pakistan, India, Tibet and as far away as Burma. There appear to be three distinct forms—whether they are meant to be three separate species, or one species at different growth stages, is unclear. Two forms are red, one of these is the "normal" yeti, and the other is a smaller version, although this could simply be a juvenile. The third form is a taller creature, which has black hair, but this does not necessarily mean that it is a different species—as an illustration of this, take a look at male silverback gorillas, for instance.

The legend of Bigfoot comes from the American northwest, where there have been hundreds of reports of a large furry primate walking on two legs, and varying between six and eight feet tall. These sightings were first made by native Indians many hundreds of years ago, and have, therefore, become an integral part of some of their cultural folklore. Some of the more southerly tribes seem to view these creatures as spiritual beings; those tribes from the more northern regions accept that this a living creature, just like any other animal. There are many native names for the creature, but "Sasquatch" is the most commonly used. The name "Bigfoot" is a modern one, coined by a journalist after massive footprints were found near Bluff Creek, in Northern California in 1958.

It is interesting to note that when Leif Erikson, the Viking, and his men arrived in America in 986 AD, they saw "monsters, horribly ugly, hairy, swarthy, with great black eyes." It is hard to know what they saw—after all, they would have already been familiar with most of the large animals they are likely to have seen—bears, wolves and so on. It could be suggested that they wanted to embellish their story with tales of dangerous monsters, but it is strange that they should have chosen to describe a creature that is still being reported today. If such adventurers were to have made up stories about creatures they met, one could have expected them to have described a beast with six heads, or something a bit more exciting than long-haired primates.

The record of sightings continued with the early pioneers and has continued to this day. The credibility of the legend has not been helped by several hoaxes, such as fake footprints, and so on, often instigated as harmless jokes. It is difficult to know, therefore, when to take "harder evidence" seriously—a good example is that of some film taken in 1967 of a creature purported to be a female Bigfoot, again from the Bluff Creek area. No one has been able to prove it is a hoax, but then again, no one has been able to prove that it is genuine. More "evidence" turned up when hair samples were found by three men in the Blue Mountains, in southeast Washington state. Hiking in the woods, they found a clearing where several small trees had been broken, and there was a strange smell in the air. On the stumps of the freshly damaged trees, they found a few long dark animal hairs. They went on to see a seven foot tall ape-like creature, and heard the screams of others.

This remains as the hardest evidence yet brought to light in the western world. The samples have been analyzed using DNA techniques, but the results are not conclusive. There are many questions to be answered—especially concerning the number of footprints that seem to have come from such remote areas; it is highly unlikely that they could have been faked.

There is a long history of ape-man records in the former Soviet Union, many of them centered on the southern Central Asian mountains of Pamir, where the local Russians refer to the unidentified creature as *Snezhni Chelovyek*, or "Snow Person." The Caucasus region also has had claimed sightings, including one by an army doctor in 1941.

The most interesting story is that of Major-General Mikhail Stephanovich Topilsky, commissar of a mounted regiment in the war against the White Russians. It was while he was with his men in the Pamir mountains that there was an encounter with some strange ape-men. Some White Russians had taken refuge in a cliff-cave in the middle of a glacier, when the pursuers heard gunfire. They thought it was directed at them, but then part of the glacier collapsed and, in the ensuing snowfall, one of the bandits was captured. He told them that while they were in the cave, they had been attacked by some strange ape-men, who came at them howling and waving big sticks. The bandits tried to escape by shooting their way out, but one of them was killed by the creatures. The surviving bandit received a shoulder injury from one of the stick-wielding ape-men, before he managed to shoot the creature dead.

Topilsky then had his men dig up the body of the ape-man, which had three bullet wounds. It seemed like an ape at first, being covered with hair, but it looked like a man. The army doctor made a thorough inspection of the corpse. The doctor decided it was non-human, about 5ft 7in tall, and quite old. It had no facial hair, powerful eyebrows, a massive jawbone, and thick matted hair. Modern scientists who have studied the facts as recorded have deduced that the creature was a Neanderthal. The director of the Modern History Department of Moscow Academy, Professor Boris Porshnev has stated that to suggest that all Neanderthals died out within 3,000 years of each other is "biologically absurd," and that it is entirely possible that the hundreds of years of wildman sightings in the Mongolian region were simply descendants of the Neanderthals—although another authoritative academic, Professor John Napier, has commented on the subject saying, "It is not impossible that pockets of Neanderthals living in geographically remote regions of eastern Europe, Siberia and Mongolia could have avoided the consequences of either physical extermination or racial absorption and still be surviving as relict populations in these regions today."

Footprints of the Abominable Snowman? This 1951 photograph taken on the slopes of Mount Everest, purports to show the track of a yeti.

Another country with a tradition of ape-man sightings is China. From the remotest parts have come many hundreds of reports, with some local people claiming to have traded goods with them, and others claiming to have samples of their hair. One of the more recent reports was in 1993, when a group of Chinese engineers saw three ape-men in Shennongjia National Forest Park in western Hubei province. The Chinese government even set up an official group—the Committee for the Search of Strange and Rare Creatures—to try and solve the mystery. Its members included many established academics from the Institute of Vertebrate Palaeontology and Palaeanthropology, part of the Chinese Academy of Sciences. The committee has obtained hair samples and casts of footprints, from which it has been deduced that the ape-man could weigh well over 600 pounds!

There have also been many stories of ape-men from Malaysia, where footprints measuring 18 inches have been found. The natives there have a long history of encounters with long-haired giant men, and have many names for them, including "Orang Kubu," which translates as something like "Lair Man." There have been stories of large red-haired ape-men living in cliff caves in Sumatra for many years, but even after careful scientific study, no-one has any direct evidence of them.

Similarly, in South America, there have been stories of strange giant apes—the best known of these is that of *Ameranthropoides loysi*, or "Mono Rei." The story came about when a Swiss geologist, named Dr. Francois de Loys was working in the region of the Venezuelan—Colombian border, around 1920. He and his men were surprised by two big monkeys which came out of the trees threatening them with branches—the men were frightened by their aggression, and so shot at them, killing the female. From the only evidence he brought back with him—a faded photograph—it appears that they could well have been an extinct species of giant howler monkey.

PART**TWO**

THE PRIMATES

PRIMATE FAMILIES

Above: The large eyes of the mouse lemurs tell us immediately that they are nocturnal. They are only to be found in Madagascar, where habitat loss threatens the survival of many species. This one is a gray or lesser mouse lemur.

Name: Gray Mouse Lemur (*Microcebus murinus*)
Author: J. F. Miller, 1777
Original Name: *Lemur murinus*
Distribution: West and south Madagascar

The Order Primata is divided into two further categories, the Strepsirhini and the Haplorhini. The way that the two groups are differentiated is really a matter for the taxonomists, as the distinctions are quite technical. A simplified list of anatomical features of the Strepsirhini includes the fact that they all have a grooming nail, a reflective layer in the eye called a tapetum, they have a "wet" nose, a separation between the upper central teeth, and the canines and incisors form a structure called a "dental comb" (except the aye-aye). Their sense of smell is very highly developed and, as a result, scents play an important part in their social lives. The Strepsirhini include such families as the lemurs, lorises, pottos and bushbabies. The Haplorhini include such families as the marmosets, tamarins, New World monkeys, Old World monkeys, gibbons, great apes, and humans. These families all have "dry" nostrils, and do not have a tapetum. The two groups are composed of the following families:

Strepsirhini

The Dwarf Lemurs—Family Cheirogaleidae
The True Lemurs—Family Lemuridae
The Sportive Lemurs—Family Megaladapidae
The Indris and Sifakas—Family Indridae
The Aye-ayes—Daubentoniidae
The Lorises—Family Loridae
The Galagos and Bushbabies—Family Galagonidae

Haplorhini

The Tarsiers—Family Tarsiidae
The Marmosets and Tamarins—Family Callitrichidae
The New World Monkeys—Family Cebidae
The Old World Monkeys—Family Cercopithecidae
The Gibbons and Lesser Apes—Family Hylobatidae
The Humans and Great Apes—Family Hominidae

THE DWARF LEMURS

FAMILY CHEIROGALEIDAE, GRAY, 1873

HAIRY-EARED DWARF LEMUR, *ALLOCEBUS TRICHOTIS*
GREATER DWARF LEMUR, *CHEIROGALEUS MAJOR*
FAT-TAILED DWARF LEMUR, *CHEIROGALEUS MEDIUS*
COQUEREL'S MOUSE LEMUR, *MICROCEBUS COQUERELI*
GRAY OR LESSER MOUSE LEMUR, *MICROCEBUS MURINUS*
FORK-CROWNED LEMUR, *PHANER FURCIFER*
RUFUS OR BROWN MOUSE LEMUR, *MICROCEBUS RUFUS*

Left: This rufus or brown mouse lemur has spotted something down below—by the look of anticipation, it is most likely to be something to eat, although it might have spotted a potential mate.

The Cheirogaleidae family consists of the dwarf and mouse lemurs, of which there are five known species in all. The dwarf lemurs are represented by the fat-tailed dwarf lemur (*Cheirogaleus medius*), and the greater dwarf lemur (*Cheirogaleus major*). They are larger than the mouse lemurs, with the fat-tailed reaching about 15 inches long (including the tail), and the greater dwarf lemur is even bigger.

The mouse lemurs are very small, and include the pygmy mouse lemur (*Microcebus myoxinus*), which is the smallest primate in the world. This species is a good example of how hard it can be to know whether an animal known only from very old sightings is distinct from its close relatives or not. It had not been properly studied since it was first discovered in 1852, and it was so similar to the other mouse lemurs that many thought it was a subspecies. It took the dedicated work of two German scientists from the Primate Center in Gottingen to re-establish the credentials of the pygmy mouse lemur. In 1992, they found several specimens, and by taxonomic comparisons concluded that it was not the same as either the gray mouse lemur (*Microcebus murinus*) or the rufus (or brown) mouse lemur (*Microcebus rufus*), with which it had previously been confused.

THE TRUE LEMURS

FAMILY LEMURIDAE, GRAY, 1821

BAMBOO LEMURS

GENUS HAPALEMUR

EASTERN LESSER BAMBOO LEMUR, *HAPALEMUR GRISEUS GRISEUS*
GOLDEN BAMBOO LEMUR, *HAPALEMUR AUREUS*
GREATER BAMBOO LEMUR, *HAPALEMUR SIMUS*
LAC ALAOTRA BAMBOO LEMUR, *HAPALEMUR GRISEUS ALAOTRENSIS*
LESSER BAMBOO LEMUR, *HAPALEMUR GRISEUS*
WESTERN LESSER BAMBOO LEMUR, *HAPALEMUR GRISEUS OCCIDENTALIS*

BROWN LEMURS

GENUS EULEMUR

BLACK LEMUR, *EULEMUR MACACO MACACO*
BLUE-EYED BLACK LEMUR, *EULEMUR MACACO FLAVIFRONS*
BROWN LEMUR, *EULEMUR FULVUS*
COLLARED BROWN LEMUR, *EULEMUR FULVUS COLLARIS*
COMMON BROWN LEMUR, *EULEMUR FULVUS FULVUS*
CROWNED LEMUR, *EULEMUR CORONATUS*
MONGOOSE LEMUR, *EULEMUR MONGOZ*
RED-BELLIED LEMUR, *EULEMUR RUBRIVENTER*
RED-FRONTED BROWN LEMUR, *EULEMUR FULVUS RUFUS*
SANFORD'S BROWN LEMUR, *EULEMUR FULVUS SANFORDI*
WHITE-FRONTED BROWN LEMUR, *EULEMUR FULVUS ALBIFRONS*
WHITE-COLLARED BROWN LEMUR, *EULEMUR FULVUS ALBOCOLLARIS*

RING-TAILED LEMURS

GENUS LEMUR

RING-TAILED LEMUR, *LEMUR CATTA*

RUFUS LEMURS

GENUS VARECIA

RUFFED LEMURS, *VARECIA VARIEGATA*
BLACK-AND-WHITE RUFFED LEMUR, *VARECIA VARIEGATA VARIEGATA*
RED RUFFED LEMUR, *VARECIA VARIEGATA RUBRA*

The Lemuridae family consists of the true lemurs. These are restricted to the Indian Ocean island of Madagascar, where many of them are desperately endangered, mostly through deforestation.

There are four genera and ten species of true lemurs currently recognized, although there are 23 when you include subspecies. (The currently recognized genera, species, and subspecies are shown on page 40.) How the species and subspecies are separated is bound to change, as several of them are on the borderline of being considered distinct in their own right. Modern technology is certain to throw new light on this subject through the use of things like DNA testing, which will probably cause more heated discussion among the taxonomists!

A good example of how difficult this business of sorting out which animals belong where is that of the red-ruffed lemur and the black-and-white ruffed lemur, which seem at first examination to be completely different, especially as they behave differently as well. They are, however, currently placed as subspecies of the same animal.

Above: The true lemurs are a fascinating family of desperately endangered primates only found on the Indian Ocean island of Madagascar. The ring-tailed lemur is probably the best-known of the many species.

Right: When lemurs have young, they have to take them with them on their travels. This female red-fronted brown lemur has a week-old infant clinging to her fur. It is amazing just how such a small creature can grasp securely to its mother when she is moving from tree to tree. One hopes that she makes allowances for her young passenger!

Below Right: Some of the different species and subspecies of the brown lemur genus vary considerably in coloration, although many are so similar as to defy identification without detailed examination. This individual is a brown lemur.

Far Right: This crowned lemur appropriately appears to have found itself a throne from which to survey its kingdom. The structure it is sitting on is a natural geological feature called a limestone "karst."

Name: Gentle Lemurs, Bamboo Lemurs (*Hapalemur*)

Author: I. Geoffroy, 1851

Original Name: *Lemur*

Distribution: Madagascar

Name: Brown Lemur—*Eulemur fulvus*

Author: C9. Geoffroy, 1796

Original Name: *Lemur fulvus*

Distribution: Coastal Madagascar, except extreme south; Mayotte (Comoro Islands)

Name: Crowned Lemur—*Eulemur coronatus*

Author: Gray, 1842

Original Name: *Lemur coronatus*

Distribution: Mt. Ambre (North Madagascar)

Left: Like all the members of her family, this female black lemur is supremely adapted to life in the trees. Here, she is seen foraging for leaves in the rain forests of northwest Madagascar.

Far Left: Something has caught the attention of this pair of female black lemurs—maybe it's merely a friendly cry by one of their family group, but judging by their postures, it's more likely to be a warning call, perhaps from another lemur, or maybe from a bird of some kind.

Left: Ring-tailed lemurs, as with most members of the family, have a habit of sitting on their haunches. For this one it is a convenient position in which to suckle her infant.

Far Left: When they are sleeping, ring-tailed lemurs curl into a ball with their tail over their head.

STREPSIRHINI

THE SPORTIVE LEMURS

FAMILY MEGALADAPIDAE, MAJOR, 1893

GRAY-BACKED SPORTIVE LEMUR, *LEPILEMUR DORSALIS*
MILNE-EDWARDS SPORTIVE LEMUR, *LEPILEMUR EDWARDSI*
WHITE-FOOTED SPORTIVE LEMUR, *LEPILEMUR LEUCOPUS*
SMALL-TOOTHED SPORTIVE LEMUR, *LEPILEMUR MICRODON*
WEASEL SPORTIVE LEMUR, *LEPILEMUR MUSTELINUS*
RED-TAILED SPORTIVE LEMUR, *LEPILEMUR RUFICAUDATUS*
NORTHERN SPORTIVE LEMUR, *LEPILEMUR SEPTENTIRONALIS*

Name: White-footed Sportive Lemur—*Lepilemur leucopus*
Author: Major, 1894
Original Name: *Lepidolemur leucopus*
Distribution: Arid zone of south Madagascar

The Megaladapidae family are only found in Madagascar, and consist of the "sportive" or giant lemurs. These are quite large nocturnal animals, which are arboreal—moving through the forest at high speed by leaping from tree to tree. They are particularly good at this because they have binocular vision, which means that they have both eyes situated on the front of the face, like we do, rather than at the sides, like say, a dog. This gives them the ability to judge distances more accurately, which is vitally important when making long jumps high above the ground.

They are primarily folivorous—that is, they eat the foliage of various trees and plants. They will, however, eat flowers and fruits as well when the opportunity presents itself. The males are highly territorial, and make it well known to the whole forest just where their boundaries are by making extremely loud calls, warning off any other males in the vicinity. Should any of them decide to encroach, the resident male will respond in a violently aggressive manner. The males are solitary, but may have several females within their territory, each of whom will live with her singly born offspring.

The sportive lemurs are all endangered species, with land encroachment yet again being the biggest threat to their survival.

Above Right: This white-footed sportive lemur is doing what most of this nocturnal family do during the day—it is resting. These large animals are all endangered due to habitat loss caused by mankind. They mostly eat leaves, although they will also take flowers and fruits as they forage through their large territories.

Below Right: The large eyes and long fingers on this white-footed sportive lemur show how well they are adapted to feeding at night on leaves and fruit—their ears are small, indicating that they do not need acute hearing in order to find food.

STREPSIRHINI

THE INDRIS & SIFAKAS

FAMILY INDRIDAE, BURNETT, 1828

AVAHI, *AVAHI LANIGER*
INDRI, *INDRI INDRI*
DIADEMED SIFAKA, *PROPITHECUS DIADEMA*
VERREAUX'S SIFAKA, *PROPITHECUS VERREAUXI*

Name: Diademed Sifaka—*Propithecus diadema*
Author: Bennett, 1832
Original Name: *Propithecus diadema*
Distribution: North and east Madagascar

The Indridae family consists of the indris and sifakas—the indris are the largest members of the lemur family, with body weights sometimes exceeding 15 pounds. The diademed sifaka also comes close to this size—they are named after their cry, which sounds like "sifaka." The indris are an extremely endangered species; particularly so, as no one has successfully kept them in captivity, let alone managed to breed them. There are many reasons for this, not the least of which is that they require large ranges—they are well known for their incredibly loud vocalizations which will often be answered by others up to two miles away! The sifakas are likewise almost impossible to breed in captivity.

There are many threats to the survival of these fascinating creatures—the primary one being that which we hear so often, that of habitat destruction by land-hungry humans. They live in the beautiful rain forests of eastern Madagascar, which are daily being depleted in the hunt for farming land and timber. They are also eaten by many people, some of whom regard them as a delicacy, which is a sad end for these gentle foliage-eaters.

The sifakas, as with so many primates, are not easy to categorize taxonomically—there are several subspecies of the three currently recognized species. These are the golden-crowned sifaka (*Propithecus tattersalli*), the diademed sifaka (*Propithecus diadema*), and Verreaux's sifaka (*Propithecus verreauxi*). Coquerel's sifaka (*Propithecus verreauxi coquereli*) is a subspecies of Verreaux's sifaka, for instance.

Above: Many primate species are very similar to one another, so it can be very difficult to decide scientifically when to call an animal a species, or a subspecies. This one, for instance, is called Coquerel's sifaka, which is a subspecies of Verreaux's sifaka.

Right: The diademed sifaka is a beautifully colored creature, which—like all other members of its family—lives only in the rainforests of Madagascar.

STREPSIRHINI

THE AYE-AYES

FAMILY DAUBENTONIIDAE, GRAY, 1863

Name: Aye-aye—*Daubentonia madagascariensis*

Author: (Gmelin, 1788)

Original Name: *Sciurus madagascariensis*

Distribution: North-east and north-west Madagascar (discontinuous)

Above Right: Close-up, the aye-aye really does look very strange indeed—the reason for this is that it is supremely adapted to its ecological niche. It hunts at night among rotting timber for the larvae of certain wood-boring insects. It needs such big ears because it listens out for anything moving within the dead wood, and then it uses a very long middle finger to prize the reluctant larva out of its hole.

Below Right: As with all nocturnal primates, the aye-aye has massive eyes so that it can find its way around in almost total darkness. It lives in the rain forests of Madagascar, where it is becoming increasingly rare.

The Daubentoniidae cannot really be called a family as such, as it only contains one living species. It is, however, one of the oddest and most interesting of all the animals in the world—the aye-aye (*Daubentonia madagascariensis*). During the 1800s, many scientists thought that the aye-aye should be classified as a rodent due to its strange dental layout, which is unlike that of any other primate. Its appearance is very strange, having large ears and long middle fingers. It has this highly unusual structure because it hunts at night, using its excellent hearing to locate the wood-boring insect larvae which are its prey. These are usually the larvae of certain moths, beetles, and wasps which live in dead tree trunks. It then uses its long middle fingers to extricate these tasty morsels from the decaying wood, and then devours them. The aye-aye also feeds off fungi, nectar, and fruit seeds.

While the aye-aye is the largest of the nocturnal primates, fossil remains suggest that there was once a much larger relative which lived on the island of Madagascar. It was almost certainly hunted to extinction by mankind, and may have been up to five times heavier than the aye-aye, which accounts for its Latin name—*Daubentonia robusta*. Over the years their strange looks have fostered all sorts of folklore beliefs: that they possess strange demonic powers; to see one was a portent of doom, or that they could invoke curses on the hapless local people.

STREPSIRHINI

THE LORISES

FAMILY LORIDAE, GRAY, 1821

GENUS NYCTICEBUS

SLOW LORIS, *NYCTICEBUS COUCANG*
PYGMY SLOW LORIS, *NYCTICEBUS PYGMAEUS*

GENUS LORISIDAE

SLENDER LORIS, *LORIS TARDIGRADUS*

GENUS PERODICTICUS

POTTO, *PERODICTICUS POTTO*, M. FCLLER, 1766

GENUS ARCTOCEBUS

ANGWANTIBO, OR CALABAR ANGWANTIBO, *ARCTOCEBUS CALABARENSIS*
GOLDEN ANGWANTIBO, *ARCTOCEBUS AUREUS*

Name: Greater Slow Loris—*Nycticebus coucang*
Author: Boddaert, 1785 (*Tardigradus coucang*)
Vernacular Name: Kukang; Malu-malu
Distribution: Sumatra, Riau and Natuna Islands, Bangka, Kalimantan and Java
Ecology: Forests; arboreal; nocturnal

Right: This slow loris has found a hole in a tree in which to lie-up during the day—this will keep it out of the way of most of its predators—including such things as eagles and monkeys.

The Loridae family consists of the lorises, the pottos, and the angwantibos. They are tail-less primates that live throughout the southeast Asian region. Superficially, they look very similar to the bushbabies and galagos—being nocturnal, they also have huge eyes, and fur suitable for keeping warm at night. They live in very similar forested habitats, although they come from very different parts of the world. They do differ from the bushbabies in one major way, though, and that is that they move much more slowly, creeping upon their prey in a covert manner. This quiet, cautious movement also helps them to avoid being noticed by their predators, so it serves a doubly useful function. Although they move slowly when looking for food, once they find it they can move tremendously fast, snatching their prey before it is aware that it is on the menu.

Sadly, as with most of the other primates, their biggest enemy is, of course, mankind. Not only are so many forests being cut down that there is a real risk to them from habitat loss, but some of the members of the Loridae family are actively hunted for use in traditional medicines. They are also popular as pets, being hunted for this purpose almost everywhere that they live. All these "uses" by mankind put a lot of pressure on them, with survival of the various species never assumed.

The four genera and six currently recognized species are shown above.

THE GALAGOS & BUSHBABIES

FAMILY GALAGONIDAE, GRAY, 1825

LESSER BUSHBABIES
GENUS GALAGO

ALLEN'S GALAGO, *GALAGO ALLENI*
MATSCHIE'S GALAGO, *GALAGO MATSCHIEI*
LESSER GALAGO OR LESSER BUSHBABY, *GALAGO SENEGALENSIS*
SOMALI GALAGO, *GALAGO GALLARUM*
LESSER BUSHBABY, *GALAGO MOHOLI*

DWARF BUSHBABIES
GENUS GALAGOIDES (ALSO CALLED HEMIGALAGO)

DEMIDOFF'S OR DWARF GALAGO (OR BUSHBABY), *GALAGOIDES DEMIDOFF*
ZANZIBAR GALAGO, *GALAGOIDES ZANZIBARICUS*

NEEDLE-CLAWED BUSHBABIES
GENUS EUOTICUS

WESTERN NEEDLE-CLAWED GALAGO, *EUOTICUS ELEGANTULUS*
NORTHERN NEEDLE-CLAWED BUSHBABY, *EUOTICUS PALLIDUS*

GREATER GALAGOS
GENUS OTOLEMUR

BROWN OR GARNETT'S GALAGO (OR BUSHBABY), *OTOLEMUR GARNETTII*
THICK-TAILED GALAGO, *OTOLEMUR CRASSICAUDATUS*

Name: Greater Galagos—*Otolemur*
Author: Coquerel, 1859
Original Name: *Galago*
Distribution: East and South Africa

Name: Dwarf Bushbabies—*Galagoides*
Author: A. Smith, 1833
Original Name: *Galago*
Distribution: Forest regions of sub-Saharan Africa

Right: The bushbaby's long tail helps it to balance while running and jumping through the trees. This, combined with powerful hind legs and excellent night vision, makes it superbly adapted for a nocturnal life in the African rain forests.

The Galagonidae family consists of the galagos and bushbabies. These are incredibly endearing, nocturnal animals, with huge eyes that seem to express permanent bewilderment and surprise. They are covered in soft dense fur, which can vary from brown through to silver. All the galagos and bushbabies are arboreal; that is, they live in trees, where they are able to leap long distances in their hunt for food. They eat primarily insects like grasshoppers, but they also eat things like birds' eggs, fruit, tree gum, flowers and seeds. They are nocturnal, and when foraging, do so singly, or in small groups. When they are sleeping up during the day, however, they congregate in larger numbers in safe places, such as hollow trees or old birds' nests.

They live throughout most of sub-Saharan Africa, where there is suitable forest or thick bush, but their range does not reach as far as Madagascar. Most females of the family produce either one or two offspring each year, which they then nurse until they are about three and a half months old. The lifespan of most of the Galagonidae family is around ten years. The main threat to all the members of this family is through loss of habitat, which is yet again directly attributable to the ravages of mankind.

The largest member of the family is the thick-tailed galago (*Otolemur crassicaudatus*), which can reach nearly 33 inches long (including the tail). They all come from south of the Saharan desert, in Africa. The four genera and 11 species are shown above.

HAPLORHINI

THE TARSIERS

FAMILY TARSIIDAE, GRAY, 1825

HORSFIELD'S TARSIER, *TARSIUS BANCANUS*
DIAN'S TARSIER, *TARSIUS DIANAE*
PYGMY TARSIER, *TARSIUS PUMILUS*
SPECTRAL TARSIER, *TARSIUS SPECTRUM*
PHILIPPINE TARSIER, *TARSIUS SYRICHTA*

Name: Horsfield's, Bornean or Western Tarsier—*Tarsius bancanus*
Author: Horsfield, 1821
Original Name: *Tarsius bancanus*
Distribution: Indonesia: Bangka Island, Sumatra, Karimata Island, Billiton Island, and Sirhassen Island (South Natuna Isls); Borneo

Right: This Philippine tarsier is showing many of the anatomical features that characterize the family—it has the eyes of a nocturnally active animal, and the large ears of a hunter. The most remarkable thing about the tarsiers, though, are their fingers, which are long and thin, and are equipped with small "suction cup" pads on the tips; these allow them to climb the smoothest of surfaces—even sheer glass faces are no problem!

The family Tarsiidae consists of the tarsiers. These are a small group of nocturnal primates that live in the tropical rainforests of various islands off southeast Asia. As with the other nocturnal primates, such as the owl monkeys, bushbabies, and lorises, the tarsiers have enormous eyes, and soft insulating fur. Unlike the lorises, however, they are highly active, rushing around through the canopies of the tree-tops hunting insects and other small animals, such as lizards. They also have long tails, which makes them more like the galagos, but unlike them, the tarsiers use the tail as a "tripod leg," so that they can stand more upright.

While they are small animals, rarely growing much larger than a rat, they are quite highly advanced in evolutionary terms. This has caused all sorts of problems for the taxonomists, who still argue to this day about where they should be placed in the "tree of life" for primates.

Tarsiers are remarkable in many ways, such as their ability to climb up almost any surface, no matter how smooth it is. They can even climb up glass! This is due to the "suction cups" they have on the ends of their fingers, which allow them to move about with complete freedom in the forests. They do have to keep a watchful eye out for predators, as there are many other nocturnal animals, such as owls, that will happily make a meal out of them. The task of looking out for danger is made much easier by the fact that they can rotate their heads 180 degrees without moving their shoulders.

HAPLORHINI

THE MARMOSETS & TAMARINS

FAMILY CALLITRICHIDAE, GRAY, 1821

MARMOSETS
GENUS CALLITHRIX

SILVERY OR BARE-EAR MARMOSET, *CALLITHRIX ARGENTATA*
BLACK TUFTED-EAR MARMOSET, *CALLITHRIX PENICILLATA*
BUFFY TUFTED-EAR MARMOSET, *CALLITHRIX AURITA*
BUFFY-HEADED MARMOSET, *CALLITHRIX FLAVICEPS*
COMMON MARMOSET, *CALLITHRIX JACCHUS*
GEOFFROY'S TUFTED-EAR MARMOSET, *CALLITHRIX GEOFFROYI*
SATERE MARMOSET, *CALLITHRIX SATEREI*
TASSEL-EAR MARMOSET, *CALLITHRIX HUMERALIFER*
GOELDI'S MARMOSET, *CALLIMICO GOELDII*
SNETHLAGE'S MARMOSET, *CALLITHRIX EMILIAE*
WIED'S MARMOSET, *CALLITHRIX KUHLI*
BLACK-HEADED MARMOSET, *CALLITHRIX NIGRICEPS*
DWARF MARMOSET, *CALLITHRIX HUMILIS*

Name: Goeldi's Marmoset—*Callimico goeldii*
Author: Thomas, 1904
Common Name: Callimico, Goeldi's Monkey or Marmoset
Original Name: *Midas goeldii*
Distribution: West Brazil, North Bolivia, East Peru, Colombia; Upper Amazon Rainforests

Right: The Callitrichidae family consists of the marmosets and tamarins which are found only in the high canopies of the tropical forests of South and Central America. They are small, but highly active creatures, which hunt for fruit and various small animals. This Goeldi's marmoset has caught an insect which it is now eating.

PYGMY MARMOSETS
GENUS CEBUELLA

PYGMY MARMOSET, *CEBUELLA PYGMAEA*

TAMARINS
GENUS SAGUINUS

BLACK-CHESTED MOUSTACHED TAMARIN, *SAGUINUS MYSTAX*
BLACK-MANTLED TAMARIN, *SAGUINUS NIGRICOLLIS*
COTTON-TOP TAMARIN, *SAGUINUS OEDIPUS*
EMPEROR TAMARIN, *SAGUINUS IMPERATOR*
GEOFFROY'S TAMARIN, *SAGUINUS GEOFFROYI*
MOTTLE-FACED TAMARIN, *SAGUINUS INUSTUS*
PIED OR PIED BARE-FACE TAMARIN, *SAGUINUS BICOLOR*
RED-BELLIED TAMARIN, *SAGUINUS LABIATUS*
MIDAS OR RED-HANDED TAMARIN, *SAGUINUS MIDAS*
SADDLE-BACK TAMARIN, *SAGUINUS FUSCICOLLIS*
WHITE-FOOTED OR SILVERY-BROWN BARE-FACED TAMARIN, *SAGUINUS LEUCOPUS*
GOLDEN-MANTLE SADDLE-BACK TAMARIN, *SAGUINUS TRIPARTITUS*

LION TAMARINS
GENUS LEONTOPITHECUS

GOLDEN LION TAMARIN, *LEONTOPITHECUS ROSALIA*
GOLDEN-HEADED LION TAMARIN, *LEONTOPITHECUS CHRYSOMELAS*
GOLDEN-RUMPED LION TAMARIN, *LEONTOPITHECUS CHRYSOPYGUS*
BLACK-FACED LION TAMARIN, *LEONTOPITHECUS CAISSARA*

Name: Golden Lion Tamarin—*Leontopithecus rosalia*
Author: Linnaeus, 1766
Original Name: *Simia rosalia*
Distribution: South-east Brazil: Rio Doce south into Rio de Janeiro & Guanabara

Right: The lion tamarins are very spectacular creatures. Sadly, this has made them very popular with those who wish to keep them as pets, and it has put an added pressure on their tenuous chances of survival in the wild. This golden lion tamarin shows his impressive coat.

The Callitrichidae family consists of the marmosets and tamarins which are found only in the tropical forests of South and Central America. The marmosets are divided into two genera, Callithrix and Cebuella, as shown on page 60, as are the two genera of tamarins, Leontopithecus and Saguinus.

While they are among the smallest members of the primate order, it is thought that they are actually quite high up in the evolutionary scale. There is no doubt that they are highly intelligent creatures, and that they also have many physiological features that suggest that they are quite advanced.

Their diet is composed primarily of insects, fruit, and small animals such as lizards, spiders, and frogs, which they forage for high up in the canopies of the treetops. This inaccessibility makes it very hard to study them in their natural surroundings—however, some biologists have taken to building elaborate high-altitude rope structures so that they can live temporarily at the same height as the animals they are attempting to study. This sort of work is not for the faint-hearted, as they can be more than 200 feet above the ground, and the nearest medical help may be several hours, or even days away!

The smallest members of the family are the pygmy marmosets (*Callithrix pygmaea*), which weigh in at only four ounces when fully grown! The largest members reach the size of a squirrel, and have quite long tails—these are, however, not prehensile. Many of the marmosets and tamarins have highly ornate ears and moustaches, some of which are also brightly colored, making them look very impressive.

It is hard to say conclusively how many species of them there are as more are being discovered all the time! One of the most recent South American monkey species to be described was the Satere marmoset (*Callithrix saterei*), which was found in a remote area of the central Amazon rain forest in Brazil. There are four genera, and about 32 species.

Name: True Marmosets—*Callithrix*

Author: Erxleben, 1777

Original Name: *Simia*

Distribution: Upper and Middle Amazon; Brazilian Coast south of Amazon Estuary

Name: Callimicos—*Callimico*

Author: Miranda-Ribeiro, 1912

Original Name: *Callimico*

Distribution: West Brazil, north Bolivia, east Peru, Columbia

Name: Tamarins—*Saguinus*

Author: Hoffmannsegg, 1807

Common Name: Tamarins

Original Name: *Cercopithecus*

Distribution: Rainforests of Central and South America

Name: Golden-headed, or Gold-and-Black Lion Tamarin—*Leontopithecus chrysomelas*

Author: Kuhl, 1820

Original Name: *Midas chrysomelus*

Distribution: Brazil, coastal Bahia

Right: The golden-headed lion tamarin is a very close relation to the golden lion tamarin, and this individual shows that he is just as impressive as any of his cousins!

Above: The tamarins are unusual among the primates in that they often give birth to twins—members of most other families only produce single offspring. Without extensive knowledge of the family group, it is impossible to know whether this Geoffroy's tamarin will successfully raise twins. Without our help to limit the destruction of the rain forests that are home to these fascinating creatures, the future of any of their offspring will be bleak.

Left: The common marmoset lacks the impressive facial hair of many other species. They make up for it with comical ear tufts. Sadly, many thousands of these gentle creatures have lost their lives in the cause of medical experimentation.

HAPLORHINI

THE NEW WORLD MONKEYS

FAMILY CEBIDAE, BONAPARTE, 1831

RED-HANDED HOWLER MONKEY, *ALOUATTA BELZEBUL*
BLACK HOWLER MONKEY, *ALOUATTA CARAYA*
COIBA ISLAND HOWLER MONKEY, *ALOUATTA COIBENSIS*
BROWN HOWLER MONKEY, *ALOUATTA FUSCA*
MANTLED HOWLER MONKEY, *ALOUATTA PALLIATA*
GUATEMALAN HOWLER MONKEY, *ALOUATTA PIGRA*
RED HOWLER MONKEY, *ALOUATTA SENICULUS*
SOUTHERN OWL MONKEY, *AOTUS AZARAE*
BRUMBACK'S OWL MONKEY, *AOTUS BRUMBACKI*
HERSHKOVITZ'S OWL MONKEY, *AOTUS HERSHKOVITZI*
KUHL'S OWL MONKEY, *AOTUS INFULATUS*
LEMURINE OWL MONKEY, *AOTUS LEMURINUS*
ANDEAN OWL MONKEY, *AOTUS MICONAX*
PERUVIAN RED-NECKED OWL MONKEY, *AOTUS NANCYMAI*
BLACK-HEADED OWL MONKEY, *AOTUS NIGRICEPS*
NORTHERN OWL MONKEY, *AOTUS TRIVIRGATUS*
SPIX'S OWL MONKEY, *AOTUS VOCIFERANS*
LONG-HAIRED SPIDER MONKEY, *ATELES BELZEBUTH*
BLACK-FACED SPIDER MONKEY, *ATELES CHAMEK*
BROWN-HEADED SPIDER MONKEY, *ATELES FUSCICEPS*
BLACK-HANDED SPIDER MONKEY, *ATELES GEOFFROYI*
BLACK SPIDER MONKEY, *ATELES PANISCUS*
WOOLLY SPIDER MONKEY, *BRACHYTELES ARACHNOIDES*
YELLOW-TAILED WOOLLY MONKEY, *LAGOTHRIX FLAVICAUDA*
HUMBOLDT'S WOOLLY MONKEY, *LAGOTHRIX LAGOTRICHA*
BROWN TITI, *CALLICEBUS BRUNNEUS*
CHESTNUT BELLIED TITI, *CALLICEBUS CALIGATUS*
ASHY-GRAY TITI, *CALLICEBUS CINERASCENS*
RED TITI, *CALLICEBUS CUPREUS*
BOLIVIAN GRAY TITI, *CALLICEBUS DONACOPHILUS*
HERSHKOVITZ'S TITI, *CALLICEBUS DUBIUS*
HOFFMANN'S TITI, *CALLICEBUS HOFFMANNSI*
BOLIVIAN TITI, *CALLICEBUS MODESTUS*
DUSKY TITI, *CALLICEBUS MOLOCH*
ANDEAN TITI, *CALLICEBUS OENANTHE*
BENI TITI, *CALLICEBUS OLALLAE*
MASKED TITI, *CALLICEBUS PERSONATUS*
COLLARED TITI, *CALLICEBUS TORQUATUS*
WHITE-FRONTED CAPUCHIN, *CEBUS ALBIFRONS*
BLACK-CAPPED CAPUCHIN, *CEBUS APELLA*
WHITE-THROATED CAPUCHIN, *CEBUS CAPUCINUS*
KA'APOR CAPUCHIN, *CEBUS KAAPORI*
WEEPER CAPUCHIN, *CEBUS OLIVACEUS*
BOLIVIAN SQUIRREL MONKEY, *SAIMIRI BOLIVIENSIS*
RED-BACKED SQUIRREL MONKEY, *SAIMIRI OERSTEDI*
COMMON SQUIRREL MONKEY, *SAIMIRI SCIUREUS*

GOLDEN-BACKED SQUIRREL MONKEY, *SAIMIRI USTUS*
BLACKISH SQUIRREL MONKEY, *SAIMIRI VANZOLINII*
RED UAKARI, *CACAJAO CALVUS*
BLACK-HEADED UAKARI, *CACAJAO MELANOCEPHALUS*
WHITE-NOSED SAKI, *CHIROPOTES ALBINASUS*
BLACK SAKI, *CHIROPOTES SATANAS*
RED-BEARDED SAKI, *PITHECIA AEQUATORIALIS*
BUFFY SAKI, *PITHECIA ALBICANS*
BALD-FACED SAKI, *PITHECIA IRRORATOR*
MONK SAKI, *PITHECIA MONACHUS*
WHITE-FACED SAKI, *PITHECIA PITHECIA*

Name: Subfamily Cebinae
Author: Bonaparte, 1831
Common Name: Capuchin Monkeys
Distribution: South and Central America

Name: Common Squirrel Monkey—*Saimiri sciureus*
Author: Linnaeus, 1758
Original Name: *Simia sciurea*
Distribution: North Brazil, Marajo Island (Brazil, Guyana, French Guiana, Surinam, Venezuela, Colombia, East Ecuador, North-east Peru

Name: Subfamily Aotinae
Author: Poche, 1908
Common Name: Night Monkeys
Distribution: South and Central America

Left: The common squirrel monkey is one of the better-known species of the many New World monkeys. It lives in the rainforests of South and Central America, and typifies the family in that it is an ardent opportunist, taking full advantage of the fact that it is an omnivore, foraging across wide areas taking anything from birds eggs to fruit, insects, small birds, lizards, and so on.

The Cebidae family is vast by primate standards, containing 58 species at the latest count, spread between 11 genera. They are all South and Central American species, distributed between southern Mexico and northern Argentina. They include such diverse animals as the owl monkeys, the squirrel monkeys, the capuchins, the howlers, and many others. They are all arboreal, living high in the trees of their native forests to which they are supremely adapted. Members of this family typically have long limbs and tails, some of which are prehensile. These "gripping" tails are only found in South American monkeys—they are very functional, allowing these species to safely hang off branches and use all four limbs to gather food.

The cebids have their eyes on the front of the face, giving good binocular vision, which shows that they are more highly advanced in evolutionary terms than, say, the lemurs. Most of them are diurnal, that is, they are active during the day. The exception to this is with the owl or night monkeys (genus Aotus), which are strictly nocturnal. They are shy and secretive creatures, about which much has yet to be learned—a difficult task as they live high in the trees of their native forest homes. They are inquisitive little monkeys, and as they live in small family groups without having to compete with the monkeys which are active in the daytime, they are very gentle.

Most of this family are omnivorous—opportunistically taking advantage of whatever food source they manage to find—this includes all manner of fruit and insects, but also small birds, eggs, lizards, and so on. Some though, such as the howler monkeys, only eat foliage. They vary enormously in size, with the smaller ones only reaching 10 ounces, whereas the largest cebid monkeys can be well over 20 pounds.

Name: Capuchin monkeys—*Cebus*
Author: Erxleben, 1777
Original Name: Simia
Distribution: Honduras to N Argentina

Left: This howler monkey is taking a well-earned rest from the rough and tumble of life in the trees, and in all likelihood, from some very vocal exercises as well!

Below Left: The white-faced capuchin monkey is typical of the family in that it can move through the trees at great speed by a combination of jumping and swinging maneuvers. This not only allows them to range across wide areas, but also helps them to avoid predators such as eagles.

Name: Bald Uakari—*Cacajao calvus*
Author: I. Geoffroy, 1847
Common Name: Bald Uakari, Red or Red-faced and White
Original Name: *Brachyurus calvus*
Distribution: North-west Brazil, east Peru

Right: This red uakari looks as though he is suffering from some dreadful disease, but he is in fact meant to look like this! When they are looking for a mate, the females use the "redness" of the face to assess just how healthy males are—a pale face often indicates a malaise of some description.

Far Right: The various species of the Cebidae family all have their eyes positioned on the front of the face, which gives them good binocular vision. This white-faced saki is a good example.

Name: *Aotus*

Author: Illiger, 1811

Common Name: Night Monkeys, Owl Monkeys, Douroucoulis

Original Name: *Simia*

Distribution: South and Central America

Left: The douroucouli is easily my favorite out of all the primates! I am heavily biased having helped to care for one—they are very shy, but also extremely inquisitive. This leads to a crisis of conscience for them whenever something is going on anywhere near them—they want to hide away, but can't bear to miss out on any excitement! They are nocturnal, as is obvious by the size of their eyes, and live in small family groups. Because they don't get involved in all the raucous behavior of their daytime relatives, they are very gentle creatures, communicating with small purring sounds—a low grunt, though, signals danger.

HAPLORHINI

THE OLD WORLD MONKEYS

FAMILY CERCOPITHECIDAE, GRAY, 1821

ALLEN'S SWAMP MONKEY, *ALLENOPITHECUS NIGROVIRIDIS*
GRAY-CHEEKED MANGABEY, *CERCOCEBUS ALBIGENA*
BLACK MANGABEY, *CERCOCEBUS ATERRIMUS*
AGILE MANGABEY, *CERCOCEBUS GALERITUS*
WHITE-COLLARED MANGABEY, *CERCOCEBUS TORQUATUS*
VERVET MONKEY, *CERCOPITHECUS AETHIOPS*
REDTAIL MONKEY, *CERCOPITHECUS ASCANIUS*
CAMPBELL'S MONKEY, *CERCOPITHECUS CAMPBELLI*
MOUSTACHED MONKEY, *CERCOPITHECUS CEPHUS*
DIANA MONKEY, *CERCOPITHECUS DIANA*
DRYAS MONKEY, *CERCOPITHECUS DRYAS*
RED-BELLIED MONKEY, *CERCOPITHECUS ERYTHROGASTER*
RED-EARED NOSE-SPOTTED MONKEY, *CERCOPITHECUS ERYTHROTIS*
HAMLYN'S MONKEY, *CERCOPITHECUS HAMLYNI*
L'HOEST'S MONKEY, *CERCOPITHECUS LHOESTI*
BLUE MONKEY, *CERCOPITHECUS MITIS*
MONA MONKEY, *CERCOPITHECUS MONA*
DEBRAZZA'S MONKEY, *CERCOPITHECUS NEGLECTUS*
GREATER WHITE-NOSED MONKEY, *CERCOPITHECUS NICTITANS*
LESSER WHITE-NOSED MONKEY, *CERCOPITHECUS PETAURISTA*
CROWNED GUENON, *CERCOPITHECUS POGONIAS*
PREUSS'S MONKEY, *CERCOPITHECUS PREUSSI*
ZAIRE DIANA MONKEY, *CERCOPITHECUS SALONGO*
SCLATER'S MONKEY, *CERCOPITHECUS SCLATERI*
SUN-TAILED MONKEY, *CERCOPITHECUS SOLATUS*
WOLF'S MONKEY, *CERCOPITHECUS WOLFI*
PATAS MONKEY, *ERYTHROCEBUS PATAS*
STUMPTAILED MACAQUE, *MACACA ARCTOIDES*
ASSAMESE MACAQUE, *MACACA ASSAMENSIS*
MUNA-BUTUNG MACAQUE, *MACACA BRUNESCENS*
FORMOSAN ROCK MACAQUE, *MACACA CYCLOPIS*
CRAB-EATING MACAQUE, *MACACA FASCICULARIS*
JAPANESE MACAQUE, *MACACA FUSCATA*
HECK'S MACAQUE, *MACACA HECKI*
MOOR MACAQUE, *MACACA MAURA*
RHESUS MACAQUE, *MACACA MULATTA*
PIGTAILED MACAQUE, *MACACA NEMESTRINA*
CELEBES MACAQUE, *MACACA NIGRA*
GORONTALO MACAQUE, *MACACA NIGRISCENS*
OCHRE MACAQUE, *MACACA OCHREATA*
MENTAWAI MACAQUE, *MACACA PAGENSIS*
BONNET MACAQUE, *MACACA RADIATA*
LION-TAILED MACAQUE, *MACACA SILENUS*
TOQUE MACAQUE, *MACACA SINICA*
BARBARY MACAQUE, *MACACA SYLVANUS*
PERE DAVID'S MACAQUE, *MACACA THIBETANA*
TONKEAN MACAQUE, *MACACA TONKEANA*

DRILL, *MANDRILLUS LEUCOPHAEUS*
MANDRILL, *MANDRILLUS SPHINX*
TALAPOIN MONKEY, *MIOPITHECUS TALAPOIN*
OLIVE BABOON, *PAPIO ANUBIS*
YELLOW BABOON, *PAPIO CYNOCEPHALUS*
HAMADRYAS BABOON, *PAPIO HAMADRYAS*
GUINEA BABOON, *PAPIO PAPIO*
CHACMA BABOON, *PAPIO URSINUS*
GELADA BABOON, *THEROPITHECUS GELADA*
HAMADRYAS BABOON—*PAPIO HAMADRYAS* (LINNAEUS, 1758)
DIANA MONKEY—*CERCOPITHECUS DIANA* (LINNAEUS, 1758)
MITIS, BLUE, SYKE'S, OR SAMANGO MONKEY—*CERCOPITHECUS MITIS* (WOLF, 1822)
LESSER WHITE-NOSED OR SPOT-NOSED GUENON—*CERCOPITHECUS PETAURISTA* (SCHREBER, 1774)
VERVET MONKEY—*CHLOROCEBUS AETHIOPS* (LINNAEUS, 1758)
PATAS MONKEY—*ERYTHROCEBUS PATAS* (SCHREBER, 1775)
JAPANESE MACAQUE—*MACACA FUSCATA* (BLYTH, 1875)
RHESUS MONKEY OR RHESUS MACAQUE—*MACACA MULATTA* (ZIMMERMAN, 1780)
BARBARY MACAQUE—*MACACA SYLVANUS* (LINNAEUS, 1758)
CELEBES OR CRESTED BLACK MACAQUE—*MACACA NIGRA* (DESMAREST, 1822)
PIG-TAILED MACAQUE—*MACACA NEMESTRINA* (LINNAEUS, 1766)
MANDRILL—*MANDRILLUS SPHINX* (LINNAEUS, 1758)
ABYSSINIAN BLACK-AND-WHITE COLOBUS MONKEY—*COLOBUS GUEREZA* (RUPPELL, 1835)
PROBOSIS MONKEY—*NASALIS LARVATUS* (WURMB, 1787)
MITERED LEAF MONKEY—*PRESBYTIS MELALOPHOS* (RAFFLES, 1821)
BANDED LEAF MONKEY *PRESBYTIS FEMORALIS* (MARTIN, 1838)
GRIZZLED LEAF MONKEY—*PRESBYTIS COMATA* (DESMAREST, 1822)
SILVERED LANGUR—*TRACHYPITHECUS CRISTATUS* (RAFFLES, 1821)
COMMON, HANUMAN, OR GRAY LANGUR—*SEMNOPITHECUS ENTELLUS* (DUFRESNE, 1797)
RED COLOBUS MONKEY—*PROCOLOBUS BADIUS* (KERR, 1792)
RED HOWLER—*ALOUTTA SENICULUS* (LINNAEUS, 1766)
NIGHT MONKEY, OWL MONKEY, OR DOUROUCOULI—*AOTUS NIGRICEPS* (DOLLMAN, 1909)
BLACK-FACED BLACK SPIDER MONKEY—*ATELES CHAMEK* (HUMBOLDT, 1812)
WHITE-THROATED OR WHITE-FACED CAPUCHIN—*CEBUS CAPUCINUS* (LINNAEUS, 1758)
PALE-HEADED OR WHITE-FACED SAKI—*PITHECIA PITHECIA* (LINNAEUS, 1766)
SLENDER LORIS—*LORIS TARDIGRADUS* (LINNAEUS, 1758)
PHILIPPINE TARSIER—*TARSIUS SYRICHTA* (LINNAEUS, 1758)
PYGMY MARMOSET—*CALLITHRIX PYGMAEA* (SPIX, 1823)
COMMON MARMOSET—*CALLITHRIX JACCHUS* (LINNAEUS, 1758)
SPIX'S BLACK-MANTLE OR RED AND BLACK TAMARIN—*SAGUINUS NIGRICOLLIS* (SPIX, 1823)
AYE-AYE—*DAUBENTONIA MADAGASCARIENSIS* (GMELIN, 1788)
BLACK, CRESTED, OR WHITE-CHEEKED GIBBON—*HYLOBATES CONCOLOR* (HARLAN, 1826)
NORTHERN LESSER BUSH BABY—*GALAGO SENEGALENSIS* (E. GEOFFROY, 1796)
VERREAUX'S SIFAKA—*PROPITHECUS VERREAUXI* (A. GRANDIDIER, 1867)
BLACK LEMUR—*EULEMUR MACACO* (LINNAEUS, 1766)

Right: These rhesus macaque monkeys have chosen to use a temple building in Varanasi, India for their little get-together. In such places, humans and monkeys live side by side in comparative harmony.

SUBFAMILY COLOBINAE

ANGOLAN BLACK-AND-WHITE COLOBUS MONKEY, *COLOBUS ANGOLENSIS*
ABYSSINIAN BLACK-AND-WHITE COLOBUS MONKEY, *COLOBUS GUEREZA*
WESTERN BLACK-AND-WHITE COLOBUS MONKEY, *COLOBUS POLYKOMOS*
BLACK COLOBUS MONKEY, *COLOBUS SATANAS*
GEOFFROY'S BLACK-AND-WHITE COLOBUS MONKEY, *COLOBUS VELLEROSUS*
RED COLOBUS MONKEY, *PROCOLOBUS BADIUS*
OLIVE COLOBUS MONKEY, *PROCOLOBUS VERUS*
PROBOSCIS MONKEY, *NASALIS LARVATUS*
PIG-TAILED LANGUR, *NASALIS CONCOLOR*
TONKIN SNUB-NOSED LANGUR, *PYGATHRIX AVUNCULUS*
BLACK SNUB-NOSED LANGUR, *PYGATHRIX BIETI*
BRELICH'S SNUB-NOSED LANGUR, *PYGATHRIX BRELICHI*
DOUC LANGUR, *PYGATHRIX NEMAEUS*
SNUB-NOSED LANGUR, *PYGATHRIX ROXELLANA*
HANUMAN LANGUR, *SEMNOPITHECUS ENTELLUS*
SILVERED LANGUR, *TRACHYPITHECUS CRISTATA*
GOLDEN LANGUR, *TRACHYPITHECUS GEEI*
NILGIRI LANGUR, *TRACHYPITHECUS JOHNII*
CAPPED LANGUR, *TRACHYPITHECUS PILEATUS*
JAVAN LANGUR, *TRACHYPITHECUS AURATUS*
PURPLE-FACED LANGUR, *TRACHYPITHECUS VETULUS*
DUSKY LEAF-MONKEY, *TRACHYPITHECUS OBSCURUS*
PHAYRE'S LEAF-MONKEY, *TRACHYPITHECUS PHAYREI*
BANDED LEAF-MONKEY, *PRESBYTIS COMATA-MELALOPHUS*
WHITE FRONTED LEAF-MONKEY, *PRESBYTIS FRONTATA*
MENTAWAI ISLAND LEAF-MONKEY, *PRESBYTIS POTENZIANI*
MAROON LEAF-MONKEY, *PRESBYTIS RUBICUNDA*
FRANCOIS' LEAF-MONKEY, *TRACHYPITHECUS FRANCOISI*

Right: Through no fault of their own, it was discovered that rhesus macaques were "Ideal" for certain medical experiments. Many thousands lost their lives in this cause—the one shown here is safe from this dreadful end, for it is far from the laboratories, in its homeland of India.

The Cercopithecidae family consists of the "Old World Monkeys"—there are currently 81 recognized species, spread through 18 genera. The "Old World" in this case refers to a distribution that covers the whole of Africa, central and south-eastern Asia, and some of Japan. Europe is included, but only because of the Barbary ape in Gibraltar.

Most of the monkeys in this family are from the hot areas of these regions, but the most famous exception is that of the macaques from Japan, which are sometimes known as "Snow monkeys." These are so-called because they live in the cold mountains in the northern parts of the country, where they have to endure fiercely harsh winters.

This family includes such differing species as the baboons, the colobus monkeys, the mandrills, mangabeys, patas monkeys, langurs, guenons, macaques, proboscis monkeys, rhesus monkeys, and so on. They are all primarily diurnal, that is, daytime active, and the larger members can reach as much as 110 pounds in weight. There is a good fossil record of the Cercopithecids, with many of the extinct species being much larger than their modern counterparts.

The Cercopithecidae family is subdivided into the cercopithecines, which are omnivorous, and the colobines, which are foliage-eaters. The actual distinctions are far more physical than just what they eat; in order to digest a diet of leaves properly, a far more complicated stomach is required than for an omnivore. This is because leaves do not have much nourishment to offer other than cellulose, which is extraordinarily difficult to break down into a form that the body can utilize. Therefore, in order to extract enough nourishment to survive as a successful species, it is necessary for them to possess a highly evolved digestive tract. This can be seen in a more extreme form if you look at how large herbivores deal with the same problem—a cow has seven stomachs in order to process enough energy out of grass to survive.

Most members of this family have a solid build, with their "arms" much shorter than their "legs." Although many have tails, they are never prehensile, and most have short body fur.

Most of the family live in trees, but baboons are the glaring exception to this, with a primarily terrestrial lifestyle. The baboons do have many other features in common with the other cercopithecids, such as their tremendously complex social structure. Some species, such as the mandrills, have unusual brightly colored patches on their bodies—these are a key feature of their societal relationships. Most also have very well developed facial muscles, which allows them to establish complex visual expressions—just as humans do.

The social structures of many cercopithecids are extremely complex, and vary widely between the many different species. The family group is the usual foundation for a social system, but these can sometimes be extended to include all manner of other individuals. Many species have dominant males which can be up to twice the weight of the females, and many also have pronounced development of the canine teeth.

Name: Crested or Celebes Black Macaque—*Macaca nigra*

Author: Desmarest, 1822

Original name: *Cynocephalus niger*

Vernacular Name: Monyet hitam Sulawesi; Monyet diji; Kera hitam bolai; Yaki

Distribution: North-east Sulawesi, north-east of Gorontalo; Lembeh

Ecology: Diurnal

Name: Pig-tailed Macaque—*Macaca nemestrina*

Author: Linnaeus, 1766

Original name: *Simia nemestrina*

Vernacular Name: Beruk

Distribution: Kalimantan, Sumatra, Bangka and Natuna Islands

Ecology: Forests; diurnal

Name: Javan Langur or Ebony Leaf Monkey —*Trachypithecus auratus*

Author: Geoffroy, 1812

Original name: *Cercopithecus auratus*

Distribution: Java, Kangean Islands, Bali and Lombok

Ecology: Arboreal; diurnal

Name: Proboscis Monkey—*Nasalis larvatus*

Author: van Wurmb, 1787

Original name: *Cercopithecus larvatus*

Distribution: Kalimantan

Ecology: Mangrove and riverine forests; arboreal; diurnal

Left: There is no way that you could mistake a proboscis monkey for any other species! Their enormous nose and matching tail is unlike that of any other primate.

Far Left, Above: This female Celebes macaque shows off the distinctive "hairstyle" that makes her species easily identifiable.

Far Left, Below: One of the hazards for all animals in modern times are roads—these pig-tailed macaques in Thailand have a better chance than most, though, as at least they have the intelligence to understand the danger they face, unlike the countless millions of other creatures massacred every year on the highways of the world.

Right: This young Chacma baboon in the Chobe National Park, Botswana looks as though it's a mischievous individual! This is entirely as it should be, for life as a baboon relies to a large extent on opportunism and bravado.

Below Right: Chacma baboon groups often huddle together for mutual reassurance, especially when danger threatens. Power struggles within the group will often stimulate this behavior. Sometimes, though, as with these individuals in Botswana, it's just for a family gathering.

Far Right: This banded leaf monkey is typical of the leaf monkeys or langurs—they are smallish monkeys which feed predominantly in the trees, but when the opportunity presents itself, they will come down to ground level and forage for any convenient foodstuffs.

Name: Guenons—*Cercopithecus*
Author: Linnaeus, 1758
Common Name: Guenons
Original Name: *Simia*
Distribution: Sub Saharan Africa

Name: Baboons—*Papio*
Author: Erxleben, 1777
Common Name: Baboons
Original Name: *Papio*
Distribution: Sub-Saharan Africa

Name: Javan or Grizzled Leaf Monkey—*Presbytis comata*
Author: Desmarest, 1822
Original Name: *Semnopithecus comatus*
Ecology: Arboreal; diurnal

Right: The gentle colobus monkeys inhabit large areas of Africa. This individual is a red colobus monkey. Tragically, they are not only hunted by humans, but also by chimpanzees which go on regular monkey hunts, catching and killing them almost as much for pleasure as for food.

Opposite Page, Above Left: The silvered langur is so named because the fur of the adults is tinged with silver. The youngsters, however, have bright orange-brown fur.They can be found across southeast Asia, especially in places where there are mangrove swamps or other similar extensive forests.

Opposite Page, Above Right: Red colobus monkeys are at home in the trees—their light weight allows them to go further out on the branches than other, heavier species are able to do. This gives them access to fresher leaves, and also provides a certain amount of security.

Opposite Page, Bottom: The eyes of this Barbary macaque seem to reflect just how much cunning and deviousness they regularly show in robbing food and other items from local humans! Unfortunately some of them have become quite violent in these attacks.

Name: Silvered Leaf Monkey—

Trachypithecus cristatus

Author: Raffles, 1821

Original Name: *Simia cristatus*

Distribution: Sumatra, Kalimantan

Ecology: Arboreal; diurnal

Name: Old World Monkeys

Subfamily Cercopithecinae

Author: Gray, 1821

Distribution: Africa; south & east Asia; South-east Asia to Sulawesi & Timor (Indonesia & Philippines)

Name: Leaf-monkeys, Colobid Monkeys—

Subfamily Colobinae

Author: Jerdon, 1867

Original Name: *Presbytinae*

Distribution: Tropical Africa, tropical and sub-tropical Asia

Left: When a group of Patas monkeys stop to drink at a water-hole, it can be a very dangerous time for them, as they are extremely vulnerable to attack from almost every direction. From the air they could be taken by eagles, from land they face leopards, and from the water itself there could be crocodiles. All these predators are very fond of monkey flesh—hence, the monkey who is keeping a lookout while the others drink.

Left: The incredible facial markings of the adult male mandrill mark it distinctly against any other species. A fully grown male such as this is a powerful animal, and will fear very few creatures other than big cats and, of course, humans.

Far Left: The close family ties are obvious within this mandrill family. As it takes a long time to successfully raise a youngster, both parents will take great care of it.

Right: It's hard not be anthropomorphic about these Japanese macaques soaking themselves in the hot spring waters. They all seem to be only too well aware as to what comes next . . . sooner or later they're going to have to get out of that nice hot water!

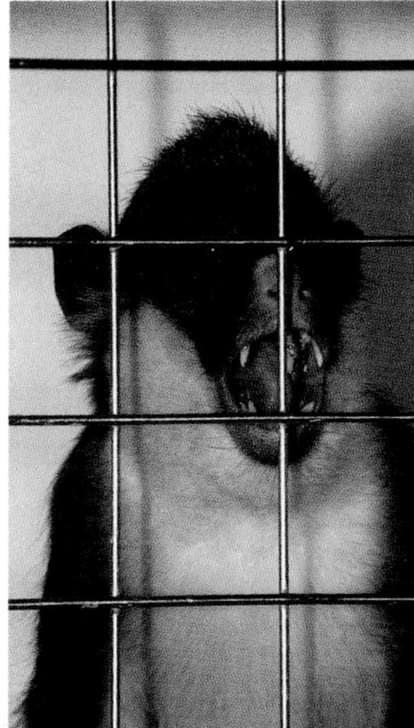

Above: It is always harrowing when you see an animal trying to get through the bars of a cage, and this spot nose or lesser white-nosed guenon is no exception.

Left: The Hanuman langur is distributed across the Indian subcontinent and into Sri Lanka, where it is held to be a sacred animal by Hindus. It enjoys a protected status there—it's a shame that more primates throughout the world aren't given the same treatment.

HAPLORHINI

THE GIBBONS & LESSER APES

FAMILY HYLOBATIDAE, GRAY, 1871

GENUS HYLOBATES

AGILE GIBBON, *HYLOBATES AGILIS*
BLACK GIBBON, HYLOBATES CONCOLOR
HOOLOCK GIBBON, HYLOBATES HOOLOCK
KLOSS' GIBBON, HYLOBATES KLOSSII
WHITE-HANDED GIBBON, HYLOBATES LAR
MOLOCH GIBBON, HYLOBATES MOLOCH
MUELLER'S GIBBON, HYLOBATES MUELLERI
PILEATED GIBBON, HYLOBATES PILEATUS
SIAMANG, HYLOBATES SYNDACTYLUS

Name: Agile, Black-Handed or Dark-Handed Gibbon—*Hylobates agilis*
Author: Cuvier, 1821
Distribution: Central and south Sumatra, South-west Kalimantan between Sungai Kapuas and Barito
Ecology: Forest canopy; arboreal; diurnal

Right: Dark-handed agile gibbons pair-bond for life, as do the other members of this family. They sing to each other to reinforce their relationship—their calls can be extremely loud, drowning out just about everything else in the area.

The Hylobatidae family consists of the gibbons and siamangs, which are normally only found in the tree-top canopies of the rain forests of south-east Asia, including Sumatra, Borneo, Java, and various other islands. They have very long arms and legs, with special shoulder joints, which allow them to swing at great speed through the trees. They are assisted in this by having small bodies, which makes them lighter, and hence able to jump further—an adult gibbon can leap 30 feet in a single jump. On the rare occasions when they descend to the ground, they walk semi-upright, but holding their arms out sideways, as though they were trying to walk a tightrope—this is partly because their arms are longer than their legs, and therefore have to be held off the ground.

Their diet is composed mostly of leaves, along with fruit, insects and eggs, as and when the opportunity presents itself during their daylight foraging sessions.

Gibbons pair-bond, that is, they form relationships for life, enhancing their social lives by singing to each other. They live as pairs, unless they have young offspring, in which case they travel as a small group until the youngster is old enough to make it own way in the world.

Name: Silvery, Javan, or Grey Gibbon—*Hylobates moloch*

Author: Audebert, 1798

Original Name: *Simia moloch*

Distribution: W Java, east to Gunung Slamet

Ecology: Forst canopy; arboreal; diurnal

Right: The arms of this moloch or gray gibbon, show well just how long they are in relation to their body size. This causes them problems when they walk on the ground, as they have to be held in the air to avoid dragging in the soil. This unintentionally makes them look quite comical.

Opposite Page, Above Left: The members of the Hylobatidae family, such as this black or concolor gibbon, are restricted to the forests of certain areas of southeast Asia. They are all superbly adapted to travel through the trees at high speed, assisted by their light weight and long arms. An adult can jump 30 feet in one leap!

Opposite Page, Above Right: The siamang is a daylight forager, mostly eating leaves, but if the opportunity comes along, they will also take fruit, insects and eggs.

Opposite Page, Bottom: It is unusual to see any of the members of this family on the ground—this is a Kloss' gibbon. Unfortunately, the commonest reason for coming down from the trees is because the forests have been cut down, and the only way to reach the next stand of woodland is to walk there.

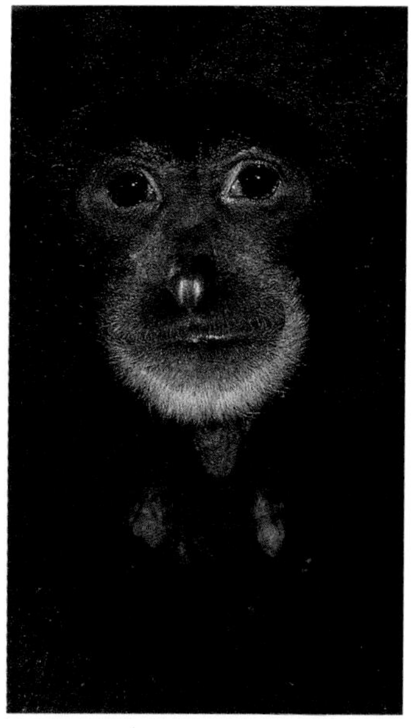

Name: Siamang—*Hylobates syndactylus*

Author: Raffles, 1821

Original Name: *Simia syndactyla*

Common Name: Siamang

Distribution: Sumatra

Ecology: Forest canopy; arboreal; diurnal

Name: Gibbons, Lesser Apes—*Hylobates*

Author: Illiger, 1811

Original Name: *Homo*

Distribution: South-east Asia

Name: Kloss's Gibbon, Dwarf Siamang—*Hylobates klossii*

Author: Miller, 1903

Original Name: *Symphalangus klossi*

Distribution: Mentawai Islands

Ecology: Forest canopy; arboreal; diurnal

Right: This is where gibbons are really at home—in the trees; this individual is in a mangrove tree where it is safe from almost anything, except humans.

HAPLORHINI

THE HUMANS & GREAT APES

FAMILY HOMINIDAE, GRAY, 1825

CHIMPANZEE, *PAN TROGLODYTES*
BONOBO OR PYGMY CHIMPANZEE, *PAN PANISCUS*
WESTERN LOWLAND GORILLA, *GORILLA GORILLA*
EASTERN LOWLAND GORILLA, *GORILLA GORILLA GRAUERI*
MOUNTAIN GORILLA, GORILLA *GORILLA BERENGEI*
ORANGUTAN, *PONGO PYGMAEUS*
SUMATRAN ORANGUTAN, *PONGO PYGMAEUS ABELII*
MAN, *HOMO SAPIENS*

Name: Chimpanzees—*Pan*
Author: Oken, 1816
Original Name: *Simia*
Distribution: Senegal to Tanzania

Name: Common Chimpanzee—*Pan troglodytes*
Author: Blumenbach, 1775
Original Name: *Simia troglodytes*
Distribution: South Cameroon; Gabon; south Congo Republic; Uganda; west Tanzania; east and north Zaire; west Central African Republic; Guinea to west Nigeria, south to Congo River in west Africa

Right: Chimpanzees are the closest living relation to humans of any known living primate. Scientists estimate that they share something like 98% of our DNA structure; sadly this similarity means that countless chimps have been subjected to all manner of laboratory testing over the years.

The Hominidae family consists of the chimpanzees (*Pan troglodytes*), gorillas (*Gorilla gorilla*), orangutans (*Pongo pygmaeus*), and of course, humans (*Homo sapiens*). The non-human hominids live only in the African tropics, with the exception of the orangutan, which is restricted to Borneo and Sumatra. The orangutan is also different from the other hominids in that it almost never comes down from the trees unless there is no choice, such as when the forests are cut down and there are no trees left. Sadly, it is an increasingly common sight for these wonderful creatures to be seen making their way awkwardly across desolated landscapes trying to find safe refuge. They are superbly adapted to swing through the trees, but don't do so well on the ground.

Chimpanzees and gorillas, however, spend most of their time on the ground, where they exist in small communal groups. A group of gorillas can be as small as three individuals, or as many as 30. Typically there will be a dominant male, known as a silverback (because the hair on his back is silver), and a few adult females, along with some juveniles and several youngsters. Chimpanzees tend to get together in much larger numbers than gorillas, with as many as 50 members in a large group.

Both species are found in tropical western Africa, but chimps are much more widely distributed, living not only in tropical rainforests, but also out into the woods of the savannah. Both have subspecies, of which gorillas have three—the western lowland gorilla (*Gorilla gorilla*), the eastern lowland gorilla (*Gorilla graueri*), and the mountain gorilla (*Gorilla berengei*). There are two subspecies of chimpanzee.

The status of wild gorillas depends on which of the subspecies is under consideration—the western gorilla, for instance, is doing quite well, with between 10,000 and 35,000 distributed across Nigeria, Congo, Cameroon, Gabon, the Central African Republic, and Zaire. The eastern gorilla is not doing so well, with only about 4,000 living in eastern Zaire. It is the mountain gorilla that is really endangered though, with only about 600 left, barely surviving in the rainforests of a small area in the mountainous regions of Rwanda, Uganda, and Zaire.

One of the biggest problems with trying to conserve the mountain gorillas is that they live in one of the most politically troubled areas in the

Name: Gorillas—*Gorilla*

Author: I. Geoffroy, 1852

Original Name: *Troglodytes*

Distribution: West central Africa, east Zaire, Uganda, Rwanda

Name: Orangutan—*Pongo pygmaeus*

Author: Linnaeus, 1760

Original Name: *Simia pygmaeus*

Distribution: Sumatra, north-west of Lake Toba; Kalimantan

Ecology: Forests; diurnal; arboreal

Right: Here you can see why they are called "mountain" gorillas; this is in the Parc des Volcans, in Rwanda, central Africa. The remoteness of their location is one of the things that helps keep these animals alive. They are still hunted, however, for fur, meat, traditional medicines, and for souvenirs for the tourist trade. Many dedicated people are doing their best to keep the gorillas alive and well—they need our support.

Below Right: This mother Orangutan looks healthy enough strolling through the forest with her youngster in tow, but how long this situation will remain possible depends on how much of their habitat can be saved from destruction.

world—when the regular brutal civil wars break out it is impossible for any conservation workers to stay in the region. The recent troubles in Rwanda represented a real threat to the survival of the gorillas there, as desperate refugees were killing them for meat, and poachers were hunting them for profit.

One of the ways in which it is possible to try and preserve a threatened species is to breed it in zoos, and then return the offspring to the wild, but there are no mountain gorillas in captivity anywhere in the world. There are, however, about 550 western lowland gorillas and about 20 eastern lowland gorillas in captivity. While it is sad that any primates are not free to roam as they please, at least the long-term effect of their incarceration is that there is a chance to breed them away from the ravages of the politically troubled countries they belong in.

Gorillas are mostly herbivorous, eating vast quantities of vegetation, including leaves, fruit, flowers, roots and fungi—an adult male will consume up to 50 pounds a day! They will, however, also eat some insects, which strictly makes them omnivores.

Chimps will eat a huge variety of foodstuffs, taking advantage of whatever opportunities present themselves. Their "normal" diet could be considered to consist of leaves, fruit, termites, ants, and small animals. They will, however, on occasion hunt down and kill sizeable monkeys—sometimes this seems to be for sport as much as for sustenance. The group co-ordination and planning while hunting monkeys is ruthlessly efficient—typically they herd a group of colobus monkeys into a situation where at least one can be trapped, whereupon it is killed and torn apart to be shared out and eaten.

When this behavior was first observed, it caused howls of protest among many of the "supporters" of the chimpanzee, who argued that it was either an incorrect observation or was aberrant behavior. The reason for this was that some people claimed that it was unnatural for humans to kill for sport, seeing our close relationship with chimps as an important parallel. Before long, however, as more and more reports were published, it became clear that it was far from unusual for chimpanzees to do just that.

Name: Gorilla—*Gorilla gorilla*
Author: Savage and Wyman, 1847
Original Name: *Troglodytes gorilla*
Distribution: South-east Nigeria, Cameroon, Rio Muni (Equatorial Guinea, Congo Republic, south-west Central African Republic, Gabon, north and east Zaire, south-west Uganda, north Rwanda

Right: While not quite in the running as a model for the next version of Auguste Rodin's sculpture of "The Thinker," this gorilla is, nevertheless, a highly intelligent creature—many scientific experiments have been performed where captive animals have been taught sign language, or something similar. The results of some have been spectacular, demonstrating, for instance, the presence of a sense of humor, along with many other abilities that were previously only conjectured.

Far Right: Knuckle walking is characteristic of how orangutans, chimpanzees, and gorillas travel when they are on the ground. This young orangutan looks worried about something—however, there are very few predators capable of taking on a primate of this size in their native rainforests, with the inevitable exception of mankind. The issue of greatest concern to conservationists is that of habitat loss.

Left: It has been suggested that the only thing stopping chimpanzees being able to use human spoken language is the shape of the mouth and throat—in other words, they can understand simple vocabulary, but they don't have the physical ability to make the right sounds.

Left: The toes of an Orangutan are also much longer than those of a human—here you can see why.

Far Left: Even though fully grown Orangutans can be massive, they can still be incredibly gentle with their offspring. This female looks as though she has mothered quite a few youngsters in her time.

Left: As male orangutan's grow older, their faces widen massively, until they look like this veteran of many years' standing.

Left: This poor little captive orang-utan looks thoroughly bored with life. While this is a big problem with keeping any animal incarcerated, it is even worse for a creature as intelligent as a great ape.

Left: It is easy to understand how early explorers came back with tales of fearsome creatures—imagine coming face to face with this lowland gorilla in the mists of darkest Africa. Those arms are solid muscle—an adult such as this could pick up a heavyweight wrestler in each hand and hardly notice!

Far Left: This fully grown male orangutan needs fear nothing at all in his native jungle—except, of course, for mankind. His facial shape, and long hair mark him out as being a senior citizen of the forest—at this stage in his life he is a phenomenally powerful animal. By nature though, orangutans are shy, secretive creatures—it is only through the severe deforestation of their native habitats that they are being forced out into the open, where they are seen desperately trying to find new home grounds. Sadly, these frightened, hungry animals, sometimes carrying injuries such as burns, react in unpredictable ways. This often leads to conflict with well-armed local villagers, resulting in many orangutan deaths.

Left: This young chimpanzee is unsure about going for a swim, and so is testing the water . . . Many animals are taken by crocodiles at the water's edge, so this is a good time to be wary.

Far Left: The ridges above the eyes on this lowland gorilla are about halfway between those of a chimpanzee and those of an orangutan, but when it comes to overall body mass, a fully grown male gorilla is the heaviest.

Left: While the ridge above the eyes is very pronounced in chimpanzees, it is much reduced in orangutans, as can be seen here.

Far Left: Life as a male gorilla is not all muscle and posture—when you've eaten your fill of plant matter, and played with the youngsters, there's always time for a bit of quiet contemplation!

Left: The bond between a parent chimpanzee and its offspring remains close for a very long time. The burden of carrying a youngster of this size must place quite a strain on its long-suffering mother.

WEBSITES

The internet has become such a powerful resource for those interested in almost every facet of human existence, that I feel it is well worth while including some of the better addresses concerning primates. It is the "nature of the beast" that the internet is dynamic—that is, it changes constantly. Therefore, it is an unfortunate consequence that some of the addresses listed below will go out of date within a short time of this book being published. I have tried to remain impartial in selecting them, and I ruthlessly removed any that did not work when I re-checked them.

As I have not had any direct personal contact with any of these sites, I cannot vouch for them in any way, other than to say that I hope you enjoy browsing through them, and that if you were not "net-friendly" before, you become so by the time you have finished!

Above: The red howler monkey is well named—all the howlers make a huge amount of noise, especially at dawn, when they shout out to all and sundry just where they are, and how many there are in the group. This is to enforce their territorial boundaries, and deter nearby rivals from encroaching on their "property."

Above Right: There is a wealth of Great Ape photography on the Internet, and gorillas are well represented.

RESEARCH & EDUCATIONAL CENTERS

http://www.primate.wisc.edu/pin/
This is the Primate Info Net from the Wisconsin Regional Primate Research Center at the University of Wisconsin—Madison. It is a resource links site.

http://www.duke.edu/web/primate/
This is the website for the Duke University Primate Center where they specialize in lemurs and other prosimians. It is an excellent site, with many excellent pictures of a large number of prosimian species, and lots of detailed information.

http://www.cwu.edu/~cwuchci/
This is the website for the Chimpanzee and Human Communication Institute, which is "a sanctuary for five adult chimpanzees who communicate with humans and each other using American Sign Language (ASL)."

SOCIETIES & LEAGUES

http://www.ana.ed.ac.uk/PSGB/
This is the website for the Primate Society of Great Britain, a society which exists to "promote research into all aspects of primate biology, conservation and management." There are lots of links to good sites and documents.

http://www.simiansociety.org/
This is the homepage for the Simian Society of America, which "is a non-profit organization founded in 1957 to improve the welfare of primates in captivity."

http://www.asp.org/
This is the homepage for the American Society of Primatologists, which is "a scientific society that aims to understand non-human primates and to facilitate the exchange of information about them."

http://www.ippl.org/
This is the homepage for the International Primate Protection League, which has been working to protect all living primates, including gorillas, chimpanzees, monkeys, lemurs, and their own sanctuary gibbons since 1973.

VETS AND CARE SITES

http://netvet.wustl.edu/primates.htm
There is an enormous amount of information available through this links site—if you need specific information about any primate problem, I'm sure that you can find it through this page!

http://mommensj.web2010.com/monkeys.htm
This is the Primate Care Site. In his own words, "This website is about monkeys and how they 'should' be kept. It's not intended to encourage the idea of primates as pets but it will help you understand the needs of primates kept in captivity."

http://mommensj.web2010.com/vetlist.htm
This is a global listing of vets who specialize in, or have a specialist knowledge of primates.

Information, Pictures, etc.
http://www.selu.com/~bio/PrimateGallery/main.html
This is the Primate Gallery Archive, a site with links to pictures, information, other websites, references, and so on.

http://www.primates.com/welcome.htm
This website is an archive of excellent primate photographs, with separate categories for lemurs, monkeys, orangutans, gorillas and chimpanzees.

http://nmnhwww.si.edu/msw/
This website is run by the Smithsonian Institution National Museum of Natural History, and is a listing of the 4,629 currently recognized species of mammals—as such it is entitled Mammal Species Of The World.

http://www.snowcrest.net/goehring/a2/primates/primate.htm
This is a primate page with sections on prosimians, American primates, African/Eurasian monkeys, and hominoids. It has excellent detailed information.

http://animaldiversity.ummz.umich.edu/chordata/mammalia/primates.html
This is a very technical site run for educational purposes by the University of Michigan, Museum of Zoology. It calls itself the Animal Diversity Web. The page listing above is for the primates, but if you want to know about other animals, the information is there, too, at the click of a link.

MARMOSETS
http://www.bergen.org/Smithsonian/MarmosetMonkey/
This site calls itself the Biggest Marmoset Homepage On The World Wide Web.! There's certainly a lot of information provided through the various links.

COTTON-TOP TAMARIN
http://www.selu.com/~bio/cottontop/
Project Tamarin is a multidisciplinary effort to help promote conservation of the endangered cotton-top tamarin in Colombia. It has sections on facts, conservation and science, a picture gallery, stuff for kids, and links to other sites of interest.

Above: As with so many primates, Javan langurs make exemplary parents—the care and affection this mother is showing her child needs little explanation.

Above Right: The only wild primates in Europe are the Barbary macaques, which live on the Rock of Gibraltar. At one time their survival was in doubt, but since a concerted effort was made some years ago to conserve them, they have proliferated to such an extent that they are now making a major nuisance of themselves in the nearby streets and houses.

LEMURS

http://www.gozen.demon.co.uk/godric/lemgall.html
This website is dedicated to lemur sights and sounds, with some excellent images, and lots of sound files!

http://www.duke.edu/web/primate/species.html
This web-page is a listing of lemur species, each of which has a hyperlink to an excellent page of information and pictures. This site is highly recommended!

GORILLAS

http://www.selu.com/~bio/gorilla/text/gorillalinks.html
Everything you could possibly want to know about gorillas is going to be available through this extensive links page somewhere!

ORANGUTANS

http://www.discovery.com/cams/orang/orangmain.html
This site is a web-cam, that is, it is has live pictures of the orangutan Think Tank at the National Zoo in Washington, D.C.

http://www.nwf.org/nwf/intlwild/oranguta.html
This page calls itself "How To Be An ORANGUTAN," and is about "how biologists in Southeast Asia are attempting to school captive apes in the fine art of life in the wild."

ZOOS, SANCTUARIES & RESCUE CENTRES

http://www.fsu.edu/~cppanama/ipsp/
This is the official website for the International Primate Sanctuary, Panama. There is a lot to see here—pictures, information about the monkeys in the sanctuary, research information for those who may wish to study there, and so on.

http://www.primate.org/
'Primate Conservation, Inc., is an all volunteer not for profit foundation dedicated to "studying, preserving and maintaining the habitats of the least known and most endangered primates in the world."

http://www.birminghamzoo.com/ao/primates.htm
This is a links page run by Birmingham Zoo, in Alabama, USA. It is an extremely extensive listing of sites about primates. If you want to follow all these up, you'll need weeks!

http://deathstar.rutgers.edu/projects/gorilla/gorilla.html
This site is entitled "Mountain Gorilla Protection," the purpose of which is "to provide a digitized database of the mountain gorilla habitat." It has radar images, digital maps, video clips, and so on.

www.sandiegozoo.org
This is the San Diego Zoo Online. The site says the zoo "is home to 1,607 mammals of 214 species and subspecies (56 endangered), 1,762 birds of 428 species and subspecies (16 endangered), and

869 reptiles and amphibians of 174 species and subspecies (6 endangered)." It is an extensive site, with lots to see.

www.wcs.org/science/wildlifehealthsci/fieldvet/oranginfo.html
This page is called "A Second Chance for Orangutans" and is about a program, sponsored by the Wildlife Conservation Society, that relocates wild orangutans to save them from hunters and habitat loss.

www.panda.org
This is the home page for the World Wide Fund For Nature Global Network. It is another enormous site that will keep you busy for hours.

MYTHOLOGY AND LEGENDS

http://night.primate.wisc.edu/pin/myths.html
This is the "Myths, Tales and Legends" links page run by the Wisconsin Regional Primate Research Center. It has lots of interesting information about Bigfoot, Cryptozoology, Wildmen, and other such subjects.

http://www.ncf.carleton.ca/~bz050/HomePage.bf.html
The "Hairy Hominid Archive" is another excellent links page about things like Bigfoot, the yeti, unknown hominoids and other related mysteries.

LASTLY...

http://www.ex.ac.uk/~pbhook
Finally, this is my own homepage. If you are interested, you can see what I am currently up to, and read about some of the other books I have written!

Bibliography

I have split the references listed below into two main categories—those intended for the general reader, and those for academics and other professionals working with primates. The titles aimed at the general reader vary greatly in technical level—some are basic introductions to primates and straightforward encyclopedias, whereas others are much more "high-brow." If you have an interest in finding out more about the fascinating world of primates, then try some of these books, (or check out the listing of web-sites shown elsewhere in this book):

General

Bonner, R.: *At The Hand Of Man: Peril And Hope For Africa's Wildlife*; Alfred A. Knopf, 1993.
Buettner-Janusch, J.: *Evolutionary and Genetic Biology of the Primate*; Academic Press Incorporated, 1964.
Cartmill, M.: "Rethinking Primate Origins"; *Science*, Vol. 184, pp. 436-443; 1974.
Conroy, G.C.; *Primate Evolution*; W. W. Norton and Co., 1990.
De Waal, F.: *Peacemaking Among Primates*; Harvard University Press, 1989.
De Waal, F.: Bonobo: *The Forgotten Ape*.
De Waal, F.: *Good Natured: The Origins of Right and Wrong in Humans and Other Animals*.
Goodall, J.: *Through A Window*; Houghton Mifflin, 1990.
Groves, C.P.: *A Theory of Human and Primate Evolution*; Oxford Science Publications, Clarendon Press, 1989.
Hamilton, E.: *Mythology*; Little Brown and Company, 1942.
Heltne, P. & Marquardt, L.A.: *Understanding Chimpanzees*; Harvard University, 1989.
Holt, R. and W.: *Primate Behavior*, I. Devore, 1965.
Kano, T.: *The Last Ape: Pygmy Chimpanzee Behavior and Ecology*; Stanford University Press, 1992.
Leach, M.: *The Great Apes: Our Face In Natures Mirror*, Blandford, 1997.
Mittermeier, R.A., Tattersall, I., Konstant, W.R., Meyers, D.M., Mast, R.B.: *Lemurs of Madagascar. Conservation International;* Washington, D.C. 1994.
Napier, J. A.: *Handbook of Living Primates*; Academic Press Incorporated, 1967.
Napier, J. & P.H.: *The Natural History of the Primates*; The MIT Press, 1985.
Nowak, R.M. and Paradiso, J.L.: *Walker's Mammals of the World 4th ed.*; John Hopkins University Press, 1983.
Preston-Mafham, K.: *Madagascar: A Natural History*; Oxford, 1991.
Preuschoft, H.: *Grzimek's Encyclopedia of Mammals*; McGraw-Hill, 1990.
Rosen, S.I.: *Introduction to the Primates*; 1974.
Rowe, Noel: *The Pictorial Guide To The Living Primates*; Pogonias Press, 1996.
Schaller, G.B.: *The Mountain Gorilla*; The University of Chicago Press.
Schaller, G.B.: *The Year Of The Gorilla*; The University of Chicago Press.
Tuttle, R.H.: *Apes Of The World*; Noyes Publication.
Schultz, A.: *The Life of Primates*; 1969.
Schwartz, J.H.: *The Red Ape: Orangutans and Human Origins*; Houghton Mifflin Company, 1987.
Simons, E.L.: *Primate Evolution*; 1972.
Simpson, G.G.: *Discoverers Of The Lost World*; Yale University Press, 1984.
Susman, R.L.: *The Pygmy Chimpanzee: Evolutionary Biology And Behavior*;. Plenum Press, 1984.
Szalay, F.S., & Dodson, E.: *Evolutionary History of the Primates*; Academic Press, 1979.
Tattersall, I.: *The Primates of Madagascar*, Columbia University Press, 1982.
Thorington, R.W., Jr., & Anderson, S.: . *Primates—Orders and Families of Recent Mammals of the World*; John Wiley and Sons, 1979.
Tuttle, R.H.: *Apes of the World*; Noyes Publications, 1986.
Vaughan, T.A.: *Mammalogy* 3rd Ed.; Saunders College Publishing, 1986.
Wilson, D.E., & Reeder, D.M.: *Mammal Species of the World, A Taxonomic and Geographic Reference* 2nd Ed.; Smithsonian Institution, 1993.

The smallest of the family is the pygmy marmoset, which may only weigh four ounces when it is fully grown! All these charming little animals seem to live their lives at high speed, chattering away at each other in a manner that is easily confused with birdsong.

Academic References

Byrne, R. & Whiten, A.: *Machiavellian Intelligence: Social Expertise and the Evolution of Intellect in Monkeys, Apes, and Humans*; Oxford University Press, 1988.

Butler, P.M.: "The Problem of Insectivore Classification"; *Studies in Vertebrate Evolution*; Oliver and Boyd, 1972.

Caro, T.M. & Hauser, M.D.: "Is there teaching in non-human animals?"; *The Quarterly Review of Biology*, 67: 151-172; 1992.

Cartelle, C. & Hartwig, W.C.: "A new extinct primate among the Pleistocene megafauna of Bahia, Brazil"; *Proc. Natl. Acad. Sci. USA* 93:6405-6409; 1996.

Cartmill, M.: "Arboreal Adaptations and the Origin of the Order Primates"; *Functional and Evolutionary Biology of Primates*; Chicago, 1972.

Cartmill, M.: "Rethinking Primate Origins"; *Science*, Vol. 184, 436-443; 1974.

Cheney, D.L. & Seyfarth, R.M.: *How Monkeys See the World*; University of Chicago Press, 1990.

Chivers, D.J.: *The Siamang and the Gibbon in the Malay Peninsula Primate Ecology: Problem-Oriented Field Studies*; John Wiley & Sons, 1979.

Clutton-Brock, T.H. & Harvey, P.H.: "Primates, brains and ecology"; *Journal of the Zoological Society of London*, 190: 309-323; 1980.

Conroy, G.C.: *Primate Evolution*; W.W. Norton and Co.,. 1990.

Fleagle, J.G.: *Primate Adaptation and Evolution*; Academic Press, 1988.

Fleagle, J.G. & Kay, R.F.: *Platyrrhines, Catarrhines, and the Fossil Record In New World Primates: Ecology, Evolution, & Behavior*; Aldine de Gruyter, 1997.

Galdikas, B.M.F.: "Waiting for orangutans"; *Discover* 15: 100-106; 1994.

Harcourt, A.H.: *Coalitions and alliances: are primates more complex than non-primates* in Harcourt and De Waal. pp. 445-472; 1992.

Hartwig, W.C.: "A giant New World monkey from the Pleistocene of Brazil"; *Journal of Human Evolution*, 28:189-195; 1995.

Hartwig, W.C. & Cartelle, C.A.: "Complete skeleton of the giant South American primate Protopithecus"; *Nature* 381(6580:307-311); 1996.

Jolly, A.: "Lemur Social Behavior & Primate Intelligence"; *Science* 153: 501-506; 1966.

Martin, R.D.: *Primate Origins and Evolution: A Phylogenetic Reconstruction*; Chapman and Hall, 1990

Palombit, R.: "Reproduction of Wild Hylobatids"; *International Journal of Primatology*, vol. 16. Plenum Press., 1995.

Patterson, F.: "In Search of Man: Experiments in Primate Communication"; *The Michigan Quarterly Review*, 19 (1, 95-114); 1980.

Peres, C.A.: "Which are the largest New World monkeys?"; *Journal* of Human Evolution 26:245-249. 1994.

Schwartz, J.H.: "Book Review of Other Origins: The Search for the Giant Ape In Human Origins"; *American Anthropologist*, 93: pp1029-1030; 1991.

Schwartz, J.H. & Tattersall, I.: *Evolutionary relationships of living lemurs & lorises & their potential affinities with European Eocene Adapidae*; 1985.

Simons, E.L. & Ettel, P.C.: "Gigantopithecus"; *Scientific American*, January, 1970: pp. 77-85.

Rodman, P.S., & Cant, J.G.H.: *Adaptations for Foraging in Nonhuman Primates*; Columbia University Press, 1984.

Wolfheim, J.H.: *Primates of the World: Distribution, Abundance, and Conservation*. University of Washington Press, D.C., 1983.